Reading the NEW TESTAMENT for UNDERSTANDING

Reading the NEW TESTAMENT for UNDERSTANDING

ROBERT G. HOERBER

Publishing House
St. Louis

Cover photo: M. Garff/The Image Bank

Scripture quotations in this book are from the *Holy Bible: The New King James Version,* © 1979, 1980, 1982 by Thomas Nelson, Inc., Nashville, Tennessee.

Copyright © 1986 by Concordia Publishing House
3558 South Jefferson Avenue, St. Louis, MO 63118-3968
Manufactured in the United States of America

Library of Congress Cataloging-in-Publication Data

Hoerber, Robert G., 1918-
    Reading the New Testament for understanding.

    1. Bible—Reading. I. Title.
BS617.H58 1986   225'.07   85-17174

1 2 3 4 5 6 7 8 9 10 PP 95 94 93 92 91 90 89 88 87 86

To Ruth

Contents

Preface

This book is written either for Bible classes or for private study. The goal is to teach a *method of study,* which we have called "reading for understanding." This type of reading is much more challenging than reading merely for information or for pleasure. It demands extreme alertness to clues in the text concerning the historical background of the documents in the New Testament. (Chapter 1 contains more about "reading for understanding.")

To become acquainted with this method of study, it is most important that the present volume be used properly. *Study questions* are inserted before the segments of each chapter (except chapter 1). These should be worked through *before reading that segment.* After working through the study questions (either by oneself or in a Bible class with the help of the pastor or a class leader), the reader will better comprehend the material contained in each chapter.

The goal is not to accumulate facts—that will come automatically—but to be able to use a *method of study* that will edify or build up the inner spiritual life of the Christian. Reading for understanding is not merely an intellectual exercise; it rather makes the study of Scripture "profitable . . . that the man of God may be complete, thoroughly equipped for every good work" (2 Tim. 3:16–17).

I acknowledge with grateful appreciation the help of two of my distinguished colleagues for reading the manuscript and making valuable comments and suggestions—Dr. Walter R. Roehrs and the late Dr. Martin H. Scharlemann. Also Dr. Ralph A. Bohlmann, president of the Lutheran Church—Missouri Synod, and Dr. Karl L. Barth, president of Concordia Seminary, read the typescript and offered helpful suggestions. Thanks are due to Miss Audrey Keller for typing the original manuscript, to Miss Debbie Roediger for putting the text into the computer, and to my colleague, Prof. Daniel

H. Pokorny, for supervising the work with the computer. Sincere gratitude is extended to the Aid Association for Lutherans, whose John W. Behnken Presidential Fellowship was instrumental in my obtaining a sabbatical leave to complete the major portion of this project.

All citations of Scripture are from the New King James Version, which I find to be closer to the original text in many instances as well as of superior literary quality and by far easier to memorize than most other translations. I also gratefully acknowledge the use of a number of outlines of Biblical books from *The Word of the Lord Grows* by Martin Franzmann (CPH, 1961).

1. *Reading for Understanding*

*T*he ability to communicate through words—by speaking and hearing, by writing and reading—sets human beings apart from animals. Unless handicapped at birth or through illness, people participate in oral and written communication with each other, and—what is vastly more important—they communicate with their Creator. Prayers, confessions of faith, and songs of praise make up the usual oral communication of human beings with God—as responses to God's communication with His creatures.

Although some people, such as Abraham and Moses, received oral messages from God, since the apostolic age Christians have depended on His written communication—the Scriptures. Today the written Word is the form of God's communication with His people. To know God's will and plan for His followers, the *reading* of Scripture is most important.

Three Types of Reading

The *reading* of Scripture, however, is more easily said than done, for basically there are three types of reading. Most of our reading is for *information,* as when we read newspapers, textbooks, and business correspondence. In moments of leisure we may relax by reading novels, dramas, or comic strips for *pleasure.* By far the majority of our reading falls into one of these two categories.

But there is a third type of reading—reading for *understanding.* Some years ago Dr. Mortimer J. Adler, professor of philosophy at the University of Chicago, published *How to Read a Book.* He expressed the opinion that only a few people ever attempt this type of reading. It is the kind of reading that he as a professional philosopher does when he reads the writings of Plato and Aristotle.

11

With paper and pencil in hand, he pauses after reading a few pages and jots down a summary of what he has read, followed by a critique of his agreement or disagreement with the author and the reasons for his opinion.

Such *reading for understanding*, according to Dr. Adler, is a laborious process and a challenging endeavor. After two or three hours of this kind of reading, he is mentally fatigued. He also admits that he is able to read only four or five volumes in such a way each year. It is not surprising, then, that only a few individuals successfully attempt *reading for understanding*.

The closest most people come to *reading for understanding* is when they read love letters. Then they read "between the lines," noticing what is omitted as well as what is written and observing even minor clues to the feeling and emotion of the writer. In the words of Prof. Adler:

> When they are in love and are reading a love letter, they read for all they are worth. They read every word three ways; they read between the lines and in the margins; they read the whole in terms of the parts, and each part in terms of the whole; they grow sensitive to context and ambiguity, to insinuation and implication; they perceive the color of words, the odor of phrases, and the weight of sentences. They may even take the punctuation into account. Then, if never before or after, they read.

Basic Questions

To read the New Testament for *understanding* is a challenging and rewarding endeavor. Certainly *information* and *pleasure* are gained as we come into contact with God's written communication with Christians. But to read for *understanding* is much more helpful—and difficult. To apply the principles of reading for understanding to the documents of the New Testament, several basic questions must be kept in mind:

1. *The author:* Is his name stated in the text (as it usually is in the epistles) or merely in the title (as in the gospels)? Are there any clues as to his nationality, education, vocation, or situation?

2. *The addressee(s):* Are there any hints concerning the type of person or persons who originally received the document? What were their nationality, status as believers, problems, deficiencies, virtues?

3. *The relationship between author and addressee(s):* Did the author know the people personally and if so, in what capacity?

4. *The occasion and purpose:* For what purpose did the writer address these people at this time? What problems or occasion prompted the composition of the document?

These four basic questions are primary in order to read a New Testament book for understanding. Four other basic questions may also be helpful and must receive consideration in the study of the documents of the New Testament:

5. *Date and place:* Are there any clues concerning the time and place of composition—early or late in the history of Christianity, before or after the fall of Jerusalem (A.D. 70)?

6. *Authenticity (genuineness):* Is there any internal information that sheds light on the identity of the writer as reported by tradition or as stated in the document?

7. *Integrity:* What do textual authorities say concerning the unity of the document? Are there any sections that appear not to belong to the original writing?

8. *Outline:* How do the various sections and themes of each book fit into an organizational unity?

Examples

One or two examples should suffice to illustrate what is meant by *reading for understanding.*

The first 17 verses of Matthew might seem at first to be merely a dry genealogy. But through *reading for understanding* (that is, by watching carefully for clues) we should see hints concerning the addressees, an aspect of Matthew's message, and a characteristic of the author.

The genealogy of Jesus is traced to Abraham (not to Adam as in Luke) with David occupying a prominent position in the first verse. What may these facts tell us about the nationality of the addressees? That they probably were Jewish Christians, of course. Furthermore, in verses 3–6 Matthew lists the names of several women—even women who were not born Israelites—and what is more, several of them had blemished characters. Since we know that the Jews regarded women as second-rate persons, non-Israelites as outside the fold, and wicked women as debased people, could the presence of these names in Jesus' genealogy indicate that Matthew wishes to stress that God's mercy extends to all nations and all classes of people? This conclusion would seem logical. Finally, we may note that in verse 17 the author systematically divides the names into three groups of 14 each. What does this orderly arrangement tell us about the author? Does it not coincide with what we might expect of a tax collector (parallel to our Internal Revenue Service agent)—a person who was accustomed to keeping orderly records?

And so by *reading for understanding* we turn a dry list of names into several helpful clues about the author, the addressees, and the message of the First Gospel.

Another example of *reading for understanding* can be drawn from the second chapter (2:13–23). Matthew alone among the evangelists records the following events:

Joseph took Jesus to Egypt (2:13);
Jesus stayed in Egypt (2:14–15);
Herod killed the male children (2:16);
Jesus was saved (2:13–15);
Jesus left Egypt (2:19–23).

When we recall the account of the Exodus of the children of Israel, we note that parallel events happened to them. They also were taken to Egypt by Joseph, stayed in Egypt, saw their male children killed by Pharaoh, knew that Moses as a child was saved, and finally escaped from Egypt.

What does this parallelism mean? A *reading for understanding* makes more of these verses in Matthew than merely another incident in the life of the infant Jesus. They are especially interesting because none of the other evangelists mention these events. This suggests that Matthew is presenting Jesus to his Jewish Christian readers as the Leader of a New Israel, the Christian church, just as Moses was the leader of the old Israel.

Thus, through *reading for understanding* the Scriptures become alive, and the message shines forth with greater brilliance. To develop this type of *reading for understanding*, one should work through the respective study questions, either alone or in a Bible class, *before* reading the segment of the text that follows (and contains the answers). By faithfully following this procedure, the student gradually will become more adept at *reading for understanding*. The goal is not to accumulate facts but to develop a *method of study* that will aid the spiritual growth of Christians.

God's Grace

While the 66 documents of the Scriptures were composed over a period of about 1,500 years (from Moses to the apostle John), the central theme of the entire Scriptures is *God's grace*—how He deals with His followers in mercy. Other terms may also be used to describe the underlying theme of Scripture, such as Law and Gospel and God's covenants—the Old Covenant (Testament) and the New Covenant (Testament). But *God's grace* is most appropriate, for it points particularly to the favor that God bestows on His followers, to His mercy, and to His undeserved love toward sinful, rebellious humanity. As we discuss each book of the New Testament, therefore, we should observe how it relates to the underlying theme of all the Scriptures—*God's grace*.

The Fullness of Time

The pivotal point of the New Testament, of course, is the sending of Jesus Christ into the world for our redemption. This event occurred, according to St. Paul, "when the fullness of time had come" (Gal. 4:4). That is, Jesus was born at just the right time in history, after God had directed the course of secular events to prepare for the birth of His Son. God used His kingdom of power to serve His kingdom of grace.

A clue to the meaning of the phrase *fullness of time* is found in the superscription on Jesus' cross, which appeared in three languages: Latin, Greek, and Hebrew. To see God's hand in history, preparing the world for the coming of Jesus and the spread of the Gospel, it is helpful to look briefly at the history of the people who used these three languages: Romans, Greeks, and Jews.

Romans

At the time of Jesus' birth the Roman Empire controlled all the countries along the coasts of the Mediterranean Sea. The subject countries were called provinces and were under the supervision of provincial governors sent out each year by the Emperor or the Senate. Some of the provinces mentioned in the New Testament are Achaia (southern Greece), Macedonia (northern Greece), Asia (western Turkey), Cilicia (southern Turkey), and Syria (north of Palestine). Roman control of the countries around the Mediterranean Sea meant that there was peace in this part of the world, a situation called *Pax Romana* by historians.

15

Furthermore, no passports or visas were necessary in order to travel from one province to another since one government controlled all the provinces. An extensive system of roads existed throughout the Roman Empire—built primarily to transport military troops to trouble spots along the borders but useful also for commerce and trade by land. In addition, travel by sea was relatively safe since shortly before the birth of Jesus Rome had cleared the sea of pirates.

At no other time in the history of the Roman Empire had the Mediterranean world been so conducive to the preaching of the Good News (Gospel). God's controlling hand in His kingdom of power had prepared the world for the coming of Jesus and the spread of the Gospel. The *Pax Romana,* unhindered travel, extensive roads, and a relatively safe sea were definite assets to the building of God's kingdom of grace in the first century of our era. All the apostles enjoyed these advantages prepared by God's hand in history. One apostle, Paul, had the added advantage of Roman citizenship, inherited from his father, which entitled him to protection from violence (Acts 22:25–29).

Greeks

God's hand in the history of the Greeks, which also prepared the world for the spread of the Gospel, is seen already in the fourth century B.C. A famous leader, Alexander the Great, conquered all the lands along the eastern Mediterranean and extended his control as far as India. But Alexander was an organizer as well as a conqueror. Wherever he went, he established Greek culture and the Greek language in that area. Although his military conquests were divided among several successors after his death (323 B.C.), the Greek language became the common language of the eastern Mediterranean world. These areas were usually bilingual at the time of the apostles; the various people spoke both their native tongue and Greek.

What this development meant for the spread of the Gospel is most important. The apostles did not have to learn new languages before they carried on missionary work. Wherever they traveled, they were understood through the Greek language. The special gift of speaking in various languages at Pentecost did not have to be permanent but was probably a miraculous ability for that day alone. A clear indication that Greek was the accepted language of the eastern Mediterranean world is Paul's choice of Greek even when he wrote the Epistle to the Romans. Although he was addressing

Christians in the capital of the Roman Empire, he wrote in Greek, not in Latin (the official language of the city) or in Hebrew or Aramaic (the native language of the Jewish members).

Jews

To see how God prepared the world for Jesus' birth in the *fullness of time* in Jewish history, one must go back to the sixth century B.C. God permitted Judah to be captured by the Babylonians shortly after the beginning of the sixth century B.C. The captors transported many of the people to Babylon. When they were released, many of them settled in various countries of the Mediterranean world instead of returning to Palestine. No doubt they saw in these countries financial and social opportunities superior to the conditions prevalent in their former homeland. But the important element is that they took with them to these countries the Old Testament and the synagogue.

The synagogue began as a Jewish institution during the Babylonian exile in the sixth century B.C. Since the Jews in exile could not worship at the temple in Jerusalem, they gathered for prayer and the study of the Scriptures. These assemblies and the buildings in which they met were called synagogues (a Greek word meaning "assemblies"). After the release from the Babylonian captivity, the Jews continued the institution of synagogues in the various countries to which they scattered. There is some indication that at the time of Paul there were 11 synagogues in Rome.

The presence of synagogues throughout the Mediterranean world also meant that the natives of the various countries were being exposed to the Old Testament and its teaching that there is only one God, who is a spirit and who promised a Messiah. The contrast between the Old Testament and pagan Greco-Roman religion was tremendous, for the latter taught the existence of numerous deities who appeared in the form of human beings (anthropomorphic) and whose favor could be won through the good deeds of individuals. In other words, the Old Testament revealed God's grace, while Greco-Roman religion promoted human work-righteousness. The contrast was so great, and the pagan religion and practices disappointed so many natives, that a considerable number of Gentiles converted to the Hebrew religion, becoming members of the synagogues. In the New Testament such converted Gentiles are called proselytes and God-fearers (depending on whether or not they had submitted to circumcision).

As we read of Paul's travels in Acts, we notice that one of his first stops in a new city was the synagogue. It was at the synagogue that Paul could reach a select audience. He did not have to convince those people that there is only one God, a spirit, instead of numerous anthropomorphic deities. They already knew that from the Old Testament. Nor did he have to convince the hearers that God would send a Messiah. They already believed in a Messiah. All he had to do, humanly speaking, was to show that the promised Messiah had recently appeared in the person of Jesus of Nazareth, who rose from the dead after being crucified and buried.

And so the lesson and comfort of God's hand in history are tremendous when we consider the implication of St. Paul's statement that Jesus was sent into the world as our Savior "when the fullness of time had come" (Gal. 4:4). For centuries before Jesus' birth, God was preparing the world for the coming of the Messiah. Through the Romans He prepared the Mediterranean world politically, so that through the Peace of Rome (*Pax Romana*) and relatively unhindered travel the apostles could carry on missionary work. Through the Greeks God prepared the world culturally, so that one language was understood throughout the eastern Mediterranean world. Through the dispersion of the Jews God prepared the world in the area of religion, so that many Gentiles as well as Jews were expecting a Messiah promised in the Old Testament. God's hand in His kingdom of power served the advance of His kingdom of grace.

2. *Matthew: Jesus and the New Israel*

As noted previously, the reading of Matthew's gospel for understanding (and not merely for information) involves noticing various clues in an attempt to answer several basic questions about the author, the addressees, their relationship to each other, and especially the occasion and purpose for composing the document. In brief, since there are four separate gospels in the New Testament, we must try to see the unique characteristics of Matthew that set it apart from Mark, Luke, and John.

STUDY QUESTION 1

Clues to the type of addressees.

A. *Compare Jesus' genealogy in Matt. 1:1–17 with that in Luke 3:23–38 (especially Matt. 1:1 and Luke 3:38).*

B. *Compare Matt. 15:2 and Mark 7:2–4.*

C. *What clue to the addressees may be found in Matt. 23:5?*

D. *What deduction regarding the addressees may be made from the fact that Matthew refers to more Old Testament prophecies than the other gospels?*

Matthew 1:1–17

The opening paragraph contains several clues to the distinctive characteristics of Matthew's gospel. Jesus' genealogy is traced to David, one of the greatest kings of Israel, and to Abraham, the father of the chosen people, while the descent of Jesus in Luke (3:23–38) goes back to Adam, the progenitor of all nations. Matthew apparently was writing for Jewish Christians. The threefold arrangement in groups of 14 also points in the same direction, for the numerical equivalents of the Hebrew consonants in the name David ($D = 4 + V = 6 + D = 4$) add up to 14. Since the last group contains only 13 names, some students of Scripture deduce that the 14th generation is to be made up of all New Testament believers, the church, as the New Israel. The difference in the names listed by Matthew and Luke from David to Jesus, according to some scholars, indicates that Matthew is presenting Joseph's lineage while Luke is giving Mary's descent. Be that as it may, the orderly arrangement in Matthew coincides with what might be expected of an author who previously had been a tax collector, someone accustomed to dealing with numbers.

Another unusual fact of Matthew's genealogy is the occurrence of the names of several women (vv. 3–6), since women normally were regarded by the Jews as second-rate persons. In these cases the women were not born Israelites, and some of them had blemished characters. Tamar bore children by her father-in-law, Judah (Gen. 38); Rahab was a prostitute of Jericho (Joshua 2); Ruth was a Moabite woman (Ruth 1:4); Uriah's wife, Bathsheba, committed adultery with David (2 Sam. 11). Their presence in this list underlines the extent of God's mercy toward all classes of people and all nations. Already in the opening paragraph then, what may seem at first to be a dry list of names contains several clues to some distinctive characteristics of Matthew's gospel: It was (1) written for Jewish Christians (2) to depict the universal grace of God available to both Jews and Gentiles and (3) was composed by a writer who liked orderly arrangement. These three characteristics merit some further elaboration.

For Jewish Christians

A comparison of Matthew 15:2 with Mark 7:2–4 is enlightening. Matthew merely records the question of the scribes and Pharisees: "Why do Your disciples transgress the tradition of the elders? For they do not wash their hands when they eat bread." Matthew assumes that his readers are acquainted with the Jewish custom of washing hands before eating, so he only refers to the practice; this suggests that his readers have a Jewish background. Mark, by contrast, includes a detailed explanation of the Jewish custom, for he apparently has Gentile readers in mind: "Now when they [the Pharisees] saw some of His disciples eat bread with defiled, that is, with unwashed hands, they found fault. For the Pharisees and all the Jews do not eat unless they wash their hands in a special way, holding the tradition of the elders. When they come from the marketplace, they do not eat unless they wash. And there are many other things which they have received and hold, like the washing of cups, pitchers, copper vessels, and couches."

Also pertinent is Matthew 23:5: "But all their works they [the scribes and the Pharisees] do to be seen by men. They make their phylacteries broad and enlarge the borders of their garments." The key word in this passage is *phylacteries*. It refers to small leather boxes containing certain Scripture passages that are worn by Jews on the forehead or on the arm during prayer. Such a technical term would need some explanation for Gentile readers. Matthew's mention of this word without any additional elaboration agrees with the previous evidence that Matthew was writing for a Jewish audience.

Another clue that Matthew's gospel was directed to Jewish readers is his frequent citation of the Old Testament. While the other gospels do contain Old Testament quotations, it is Matthew who cites the Old Testament most frequently. A total of 29 prophecies are in Matthew, 10 of which are peculiar to his gospel. Although the majority are from the Septuagint (a Greek translation of the Old Testament), Matthew also used citations based on the Hebrew Bible, which he introduced by variations of the formula "that it might be fulfilled."

STUDY QUESTION 2

Clues to the message of Matthew that God's grace is universal.

A. How do the following passages in Matthew indicate that God's grace is for all nations? See Matt. 1:3– 6 (three women); 2:1–12 (Magi); 2:13–15 (Egypt); 8:10–12 (many from east and west); 12:18–21 (Gentiles); 21:33–41 (other tenants); 28:18–20 (Great Commission).

B. How do the following passages indicate that God's grace is for all classes of people? See Matt. 1:3–6 (type of women); 5:3 (poor in spirit); 8:1–15 (first three miracles); 9:9–13 (Matthew, a tax collector).

Gospel for Jews and Gentiles

Other clues bearing on Matthew's writing for Jewish readers will be considered later. For the present a few additional facts should be mentioned concerning another characteristic of Matthew's gospel: his stress on the universal grace of God—that it includes Gentiles as well as Jews. In Matthew, Jesus' birth is honored by Gentiles, who come from the east (2:1–12), and when Jesus' life is in danger, His parents find protection in a Gentile land, Egypt (2:13–15). Matthew refers to Jesus' statement that others besides Jews would enter the Kingdom (8:10–12) and cites the prophecy that the Messiah would proclaim justice to the Gentiles and that the Gentiles would hope in Him (12:18–21). The parable of the vineyard (21:33–41) suggests that others will supplant the original husbandmen, represented by the Hebrew people. In the final verses Matthew ends his gospel with the Great Commission that extends to all nations (28:18–20).

In Matthew Jesus begins His first discourse with the beatitude "Blessed are the poor in spirit" (5:3), thus including among the recipients of God's grace those who were social outcasts. The first three miracles of Jesus recorded by Matthew (8:1–15) concern God's mercy to people of inferior rank in the judgment of contemporary Judaism: a leper, a person excluded in the Old Testament from God's people; a servant of a Roman centurion, no doubt a Gentile of inferior social standing; and Peter's mother-in-law, considered with women in general as a second-class person among the Jews. Jesus even extends God's mercy to a tax collector, Matthew, who would ordinarily be excluded from Jewish synagogues (9:9–13). So there are numerous clues that Matthew took pains to emphasize that God's grace is for all people—all nations and all social strata.

STUDY QUESTION 3

Clues to the type of author who arranges his material in groups of three, five, and seven elements.

A. *Note the following threefold groups: Matt. 1:17 (genealogy); 4:1–11 (temptations); 6:1–18 (examples of hypocrisy and pure piety); 13:1–32 (parables of planting and growth).*
B. *Note the following groups of seven: Matt. 23:13–26 (woes on scribes and Pharisees); 13:1–50 (parables about the kingdom of heaven); fulfillments of prophecy: 1:23; 2:6; 2:15; 2:18; 2:23; 3:3; 4:15–16.*
C. *Note the following groups of five:*
   1. *Examples from Mosaic law: Matt. 5:21–26; 5:27–32; 5:33–37; 5:38–42; 5:43–48.*
   2. *Conclusions of the five major discourses in Matthew: 7:28; 11:1; 13:53; 19:1; 26:1. (Note also that the Old Testament contains five books of Moses and that the hymnal of the Old Testament, the Psalms, has a fivefold division as indicated at the end of Psalms 41, 72, 89, 106, 150.)*

Orderly Arrangement

The organization of Matthew's gospel in various orderly arrangements is easily recognized on close reading—giving a clue to the methodical mind of the author. Matthew tended to group similar sayings and events on the basis of the numbers three, five, and seven. We referred previously to the threefold division of Jesus' genealogy. There are also three temptations (4:1–11); three illustrations of hypocrisy and pure piety: giving alms, praying, and fasting (6:1–18); and three parables of planting and growth (13:1–32). Does Matthew's fondness for groups of three illustrate merely the working of his methodical mind, or as some scholars suggest, may it be that Matthew grouped events and sayings into three or more instances because he was influenced by the Mosaic principle that evidence is established among the Jews by two or three witnesses? It may be the former, since Matthew is also fond of groups of seven and five.

A few examples of groups of seven are the seven woes pronounced on the scribes and Pharisees (23:13–36), the seven parables of the kingdom of heaven (chapter 13), and the seven fulfillments of prophecy in the early section of Matthew's gospel:

1. Jesus born of a virgin and called Immanuel (1:23);
2. "For out of you shall come a Ruler" (2:6);

23

3. "Out of Egypt I called My Son" (2:15);
4. "Rachel weeping for her children" (2:18);
5. "He shall be called a Nazarene" (2:23);
6. "The voice of one crying in the wilderness . . ." (3:3);
7. "The people who sat in darkness saw a great light . . ." (4:15–16).

In the ancient world the number seven usually symbolized completion. We do not know how much this fact influenced Matthew. But his groupings of seven elements, as those of three and five, do illustrate his methodical mind.

Matthew's arrangement into groups of five, however, seems to many students of the Scriptures to be most revealing of his purpose. There are, for example, the five items of the Mosaic law discussed in the Sermon on the Mount: murder (5:21–26), adultery (5:27–32), oaths (5:33–37), retaliation (5:38–42), and loving others (5:43–48). In each item the contrast is between "You have heard that it was said" (or "You have heard that it was said to those of old") and "But I say to you."

Certainly Jesus is teaching His followers that the Old Testament law condemns sins of the mind and will, sins of word and thought, as well as sinful deeds. But there is more involved in the comparison between "it was said" (i.e., by Moses) and "But I say to you." Jesus may be presenting Himself as a new Moses, the Leader of a New Israel.

Outline of Discourses

The inference is greatly reinforced when it becomes apparent that there are five major discourse sections in Matthew. Five times in his gospel Matthew concludes Jesus' discourse with a phrase such as "when Jesus had finished these sayings" (7:28; 11:1; 13:53; 19:1; 26:1). That is, Matthew is helping the reader see the general outline of his document: five booklets, each consisting of a narrative section followed by a discourse. A brief outline might be as follows:

A. Jesus' Genealogy and Infancy (chapters 1–2)
B. First Booklet
   1. Narrative (chapters 3–4)
   2. Sermon on the Mount (chapters 5–7)
C. Second Booklet
   1. Narrative (chapters 8–9)
   2. Mission Discourse (chapter 10)

D. Third Booklet
   1. Narrative (chapters 11–12)
   2. Seven Kingdom Parables (chapter 13)
E. Fourth Booklet
   1. Narrative (chapters 14–17)
   2. New *ekklesia* or Church (chapter 18)
F. Fifth Booklet
   1. Narrative and Seven Woes (chapters 19–23)
   2. Eschatology (chapters 24–25)
G. Passion, Death, and Resurrection (chapters 26–28)

The division into five booklets no doubt was intended to recall the first five books of the Old Testament, also called the Pentateuch (from two Greek words meaning "five" and "tool" or "book") and the Torah (a Hebrew word for "law" or "revelation"). These first five documents of the Old Testament contain the events of Moses, the exodus from Egypt, the giving of the Law on Mount Sinai, the wandering of Israel in the desert, and so forth—extremely important events in the history of the Hebrew people. So a fivefold division of Matthew's gospel would strike a sympathetic chord among Jewish Christians, who would think of their Pentateuch and also probably of their Old Testament hymnal, the Psalms, which had five divisions, each ending with a doxology (at the conclusion of Psalms 41, 72, 89, 106, and 150).

STUDY QUESTION 4

Clues that Matthew is presenting Jesus as the new Moses and as Leader of a New Israel.

A. *What events in Jesus' early life parallel events of Israel in Egypt? See Matt. 2:13–23.*

B. *Note the events included by Matthew that parallel the exodus of Israel from Egypt:*

Matthew	Exodus
3:13	14
3:17	4:22
4:1	15:22
4:1–11	16–17

```
4:2                  34:28
5:1; 8:1             24:15–17
8–9                  7–12
```

Jesus and the New Israel

Most interesting are the detailed parallels between Matthew's description of Jesus in the early chapters and the events of the Old Testament involving Moses and the exodus. The following table will illustrate:

Jesus	Old Israel
To Egypt under Joseph (2:13)	To Egypt under Joseph
Stay in Egypt (2:14–15)	Stay in Egypt
Male children killed by Herod (2:16)	Male children killed by Pharaoh
Jesus was saved (2:13–15)	Moses was saved
Escape from Egypt (2:19–23)	Escape from Egypt

Other parallels may be observed as follows:

Jesus	Old Israel
Water of baptism (3:13)	Water of Red Sea (Ex. 14)
"My beloved Son" (3:17)	"Israel is My son, My firstborn" (Ex. 4:22)
Wilderness (4:1)	Wilderness (Ex. 15:22)
Temptations (4:1–11)	Temptations (Ex. 16–17)
Jesus fasts 40 days (4:2)	Moses fasts 40 days (Ex. 34:28)
Mount for Sermon (5:1; 8:1)	Mount Sinai (Ex. 24:15–17)
Ten miracles of Jesus (8–9)	Ten miracles of plagues (Ex. 7–12)

The sum and substance of these parallelisms seems to be that Matthew is presenting to his Jewish Christian readers Jesus as the Leader of the New Israel, the Christian church, as Moses was the leader of the old Israel. That the church became the New Israel, the new people of God, is clear also from St. Paul's Epistle to the Galatians: "As many as walk according to this rule, peace and mercy be upon them, and upon the Israel of God" (6:16).

Jesus is the Messiah predicted in the Old Testament. Matthew stresses this fact by referring to 29 Messianic prophecies, 10 of which are peculiar to his gospel. This Jesus is also Immanuel, "God with us," until the end of the age, as Matthew states both at the beginning and at the end of his document (1:23; 28:20). This Messiah/Immanuel is Lord of the church, the New Israel, which is to present the Gospel to all nations. As the Gentile Magi came to Immanuel shortly after His birth, through the church the same Immanuel goes to both Gentiles and Jews—the mission of the New Israel.

STUDY QUESTION 5

Clues to the identity of the author as Matthew, a tax collector.

A. *Compare Matt. 10:2–3 with Mark 3:14–19; Luke 6:13–16; and Acts 1:13.*

B. *Compare Matt. 9:9 with Mark 2:14 and Luke 5:27–28.*

C. *Compare Matt. 9:10 with Mark 2:15 and Luke 5:29.*

D. *Note the vocabulary of tax collecting in Matthew, but lacking in the other Gospels:*
1. *Matt. 22:15–22; Mark 12:13–17; Luke 20:20–26.*
2. *Matt. 17:24–27.*
3. *Matt. 18:23–35.*

Author

Church tradition assigns the writing of the First Gospel to Matthew, a former tax collector. Tradition also states that Matthew wrote in the Hebrew tongue (Aramaic). While the headings of our gospels are not part of the original inspired text, it is interesting to note certain clues that seem to corroborate the tradition of the church.

We have noted the orderly arrangement of Matthew's gospel, reflecting the methodical mind of the writer. Such orderliness might be expected of a tax collector, a person who by vocation had to keep orderly records of various tax accounts. His parallel today might be an Internal Revenue Service agent.

The New Testament lists the names of the 12 disciples on four occasions: Matthew 10:2–3; Mark 3:14–19; Luke 6:13–16; Acts 1:13 (omitting Judas). Only in Matthew's list is Matthew referred to as a tax collector—possibly a conscious personal touch by the writer to stress God's grace to him personally. Three gospels recount the calling of the tax collector to become a disciple: Matthew 9:9; Mark 2:14; Luke 5:27–28. But again there is a difference. Mark and Luke call him Levi; only the First Gospel gives his name as Matthew—a name possibly given to him by our Lord, as He called Simon by the name Peter. But there is another, more revealing difference in the gospel accounts of Matthew's call. Immediately after the call by Jesus, Mark (2:15) and Luke (5:29) refer to a meal "in *his* house" (i.e., Levi's). Matthew (9:10) merely states: "And so it was, as Jesus sat at the table in *the* house . . ." The omission of *his* may be a clear clue that Matthew composed this sentence— especially since in Greek the word for *the* could be translated "my."

As a former tax collector Matthew might be expected to retain certain special interests and habits. The accounts of the payment of tribute to Caesar bring out one clue. Mark (12:13–17) and Luke (20:20–26) use the common term *denarius* for this tribute, but Matthew (22:15–22) employs the precise term "tribute money" [*nomisma*]. Also pertinent is the fact that only Matthew records the incident of the annual temple tax (17:24–27). But more important is the fact that Matthew alone includes the parable of the unmerciful servant (18:23–35), who would not overlook a debt of about $18 after he had been released from a debt of $10 million. Who would think in terms of millions of dollars and be expected to record a parable of Jesus about such a huge amount of money? A former tax collector, who dealt with the combined taxes of large areas of land, would be more at home with such high finance than the other disciples. In fact, the numerical interest in the First Gospel is strong evidence that the author was a man who dealt in figures.

Date and Place

We have no definite evidence concerning the time or place of the composition of the First Gospel. The content and organization of the document point to Jewish Christians as addressees. External evidence seems to agree that the destination apparently was a group of Christians in Palestine or Syria. At least Ignatius of Antioch in Syria, who wrote around the end of the first century, gives what appear to be the earliest quotations from Matthew; he cites 3:15 in his Letter to the Smyrneans (I.1) and 10:16 in his Letter to Polycarp (II.2).

Concerning the date of Matthew there are two schools of thought. Some prefer to place Matthew after A.D. 70, when Jerusalem was destroyed by the Romans. They point out that scholars from Jerusalem then fled to Jamnia and made it a Jewish center for the study of the Hebrew Scriptures. Accordingly, some see Matthew's gospel as being composed to counteract this development and prefer a date around A.D. 85.

Other scholars today date Matthew earlier—in the late fifties or the sixties. They point to Matthew 27:8: "Therefore that field has been called the Field of Blood to this day." Since this place probably would no longer be identified thus or used as a burial ground for strangers after Jerusalem's destruction, the phrase "to this day" would seem to imply a date of composition before A.D. 70. Also, they argue, a clear distinction between the fall of Jerusalem and Jesus' second coming would have been made in Matthew 24 if Jerusalem had already been destroyed before the gospel was written.

In brief, we see that the arguments about the place and date are not decisive. It is better, therefore, to leave the questions open. What is important, however, is that the message of Matthew's gospel is the same regardless of the time and place of origin.

Message

Writing for his fellow Hebrews, Matthew emphasizes Jesus as the Messiah predicted in the Old Testament. Many Jews at that time were expecting a political leader who would set them free from Roman domination. This expectation was mistaken. So Matthew stresses in five discourses what Jesus said about His kingdom. His gospel serves as a link between the Old Testament and the New, between the old and the New Israel, the Christian church, destined to become worldwide and consisting of Jesus' followers among all nations.

The five discourse sections develop various aspects of Jesus' kingdom. The Sermon on the Mount (chapters 5–7), the first and longest discourse, contrasts some ethical standards prevalent in Judaism with the higher expectations of Jesus' kingdom. Morality is not merely a set of rules but a change of attitude and outlook. The next discourse (chapter 10) presents the missionary charge to His followers to promulgate His kingdom. In the third discourse Jesus tells seven parables to describe His kingdom further (chapter 13):

1. The seed and the soils portray various responses to His message (13:1–9, 18–23).
2. The wheat and the weeds teach that the good and evil of this life must be sorted out only at the final judgment (13:24–30, 36–43).

3–4. Both the mustard seed and the yeast reveal that Jesus' kingdom will grow greatly and quietly from a small beginning (13:31–33).

5–6. Both the treasure and the pearl show that Jesus' kingdom is so valuable that it is worth giving up everything to have it (13:44–46).

7. The net depicts the sorting out of good and evil at the final judgment (13:47–50).

The fourth discourse teaches that the kingdom of God operates by completely different standards from those of the world. There is to be no seeking of status (18:1–4), but the spiritually strong are to take care of those who are spiritually weak (18:5–14). Members of the Christian community are to practice brotherly correction (18:15–20), and unlimited forgiveness is their obligation as people whom God has forgiven (18:21–35). The fifth and final discourse concerns judgment, both the judgment on Jerusalem and Jesus' return in judgment (chapters 24–25). Some see within this discourse seven parables of warning about being prepared, since we never really know when Jesus will come again or when our personal life on earth will end:

1. The Fig Tree (24:32–33)
2. The Day of Noah (24:37–41)
3. The Householder and Thief (24:42–44)
4. The Good and Bad Servants (24:45–51)
5. The Wise and Foolish Maidens (25:1–13)
6. The Talents (25:14–30)
7. The Final Judgment (25:31–46)

Finally, just before Jesus' trial and crucifixion there is an important connection between the old and the New Israel. Each year old Israel celebrated the Jewish Passover. In Jesus' last few days He institutes the Lord's Supper. At the exodus the nation of Israel was born. By Jesus' sacrificial death the New Israel, the Christian church, is born at Pentecost, spiritually enriched by a new sacrament, the Lord's Supper. The Lamb of God offers Himself for the whole world, and the Passover is replaced by the Lord's Supper. The most Jewish of all the gospels concludes with a command from Jesus that extends God's kingdom to people in every nation.

Outline

Matthew's gospel is symmetrically constructed of five discourse sections (each ending with the same recurrent formula), which are preceded by an introduction and followed by a conclusion (passion and resurrection)—seven major divisions. Note the symmetry within each of the five major sections—deeds and words (cf. Acts 1:1).

I. Introduction (1:1–4:16)—Jesus the Messiah
    A. Genealogy (1:1–17)
    B. Beginnings—seven fulfillments of prophecy
        1. Birth of Christ—"Immanuel" (1:18–25)
        2. Birth at Bethlehem and Magi—"For out of you shall come a Ruler" (2:1–12)
        3. Flight to Egypt—"Out of Egypt I called My Son" (2:13–15)
        4. Slaughter of children at Bethlehem—"Rachel weeping for her children" (2:16–18)
        5. Return to Nazareth—"He shall be called a Nazarene" (2:19–23)
        6. John the Baptist, baptism and temptation of Jesus—"The voice of one crying in the wilderness: 'Prepare the way of the Lord' " (3:1–4)
        7. Beginning of Jesus' ministry in Galilee—"The people who sat in darkness saw a great light" (4:12–16)
II. First group of deeds and words: Annunciation of the Kingdom and the call to repentance (4:17–7:29)
    A. Deeds (4:17–4:25)
    B. Words: Sermon on the Mount (5:1–7:29)
III. Second group: Compassionate Messiah seeks the lost sheep of the house of Israel (8:1–11:1)
    A. Deeds: 10 Messianic deeds of power (8:1–9:35)
    B. Words: Mission Discourse (9:36–11:1)
IV. Third group: Contradicted Messiah conceals the Kingdom from those who rejected it and further reveals it to those who have accepted it (11:2–13:53; note 13:11)
    A. Deeds (11:2–12:50)
    B. Words: Seven Kingdom parables (13:1–53)
V. Fourth group: The new *ekklesia*, the new Messianic people of God (13:54–19:1)
    A. Deeds (13:54–17:27)
        1. Separation from Judaism (withdrawals)
        2. Communion with His followers
    B. Words: Rules for the new *ekklesia* (18:1–19:1; note that Matthew is the only gospel that uses the term *ekklesia*—16:18; 18:17)

3. Mark:
Jesus the Christ
and Son of God

An initial cursory reading of Mark's gospel reveals several aspects different from Matthew. Mark is briefer, contains no account of Jesus' infancy, stresses what Jesus did rather than what He said (with only one collection of Jesus' sayings, chapter 13, and only a few parables), very frequently writes in the vivid present tense (at least 150 times), and uses the word "immediately" about 40 times in 16 chapters.

STUDY QUESTION 1

How do Mark 1:1; 8:29; and 15:39 indicate a twofold division of Mark's gospel?

Mark 1:1

One of the best clues to the structure and interpretation of Mark's gospel is the first verse, properly understood. It reads: "The beginning of the Gospel of Jesus Christ, the Son of God." What would be the point of telling the readers that the first sentence is the beginning of the document? Also, where is the verb of the sentence? Furthermore, should the Greek word for "beginning" rather be translated "origin" and the word for "Gospel" better be rendered "Good News"? These questions have led many to regard the opening words of Mark's gospel as a title to the document. The Greek could be interpreted thus: "The Origin of the Good News, Jesus Christ, Son of God." That is, Mark is going to relate for the readers the origin or beginning of the Good News that they heard and believed.

Mark is fond of the term "Good News" or "Gospel." He uses it seven times, although the word occurs only four times in the longer document of Matthew and not at all in Luke and John. Mark twice has Jesus identify Himself and the word for "Good News" very closely: "For whoever desires to save his life will lose it, but whoever loses his life for My sake and the Gospel's will save it" (8:35). "Assuredly, I say to you, there is no one who has left house or brothers or sisters or father or mother or wife or children or lands, for My sake and the Gospel's . . . ." (10:29). Thus in the opening phrase Mark may mean that Jesus and the Good News are in apposition, that Jesus and the Good News are so intimately entwined that a person cannot have the one without the other.

So Mark plans to relate the origin of the Good News, Jesus, and to be specific about who He was, as he apparently indicates by the last few words of Mark 1:1. He was first of all the promised Messiah of the Old Testament, the Christ (in the Greek translation). He was at the same time God's Son. Mark therefore emphasizes these two points in the general division of his document. The first part treats of Jesus' ministry in Galilee and culminates in Peter's confession, "You are the Christ" (8:29). The second centers on Jesus' ministry in Judea and His death and resurrection in Jerusalem, emphasizing toward the end the confession of a Roman soldier: "Truly this Man was the Son of God!" (15:39). Thus the two confessional climaxes of Mark's document are parallel to the two claims made concerning Jesus in the opening phrase, which could with good reason be regarded as the title of Mark's gospel. But more on Mark's purpose and theology later; for the present we shall pick up on the author.

Author

According to the tradition of the early church, which may go back to the apostle John, Mark became the interpreter of Peter and wrote the things that the Lord had said and done. An ancient prolog to the gospel states that Mark put in writing Peter's preaching in the regions of Italy. An early church father, Clement of Alexandria, records that Mark wrote at Rome at the request of people who had heard Peter preach there. Since Peter died at Rome in the middle sixties, our external evidence seems to connect the Gospel of Mark with Rome or Italy about 30 to 35 years after Jesus' death. Also the internal evidence in Mark's Gospel, as we shall see, agrees with the tradition of the early church.

STUDY QUESTION 2

A. **What does the New Testament relate concerning Mark? See Acts 12:12; 13:1–13; 15:36–41; Col. 4:10–11; Philemon 24; 1 Peter 5:13.**

B. **Does Mark 14:50–52 suggest any idea?**

Mark in the New Testament

A person by the name of Mark, John, or John Mark appears in Acts and in some epistles of the New Testament. He was a son of Mary, at whose house the early Christians in Jerusalem met and to whose house Peter came after his miraculous escape from prison (Acts 12:12). John Mark was the cousin or nephew of Barnabas (Col. 4:10) and accompanied Paul and Barnabas on the first part of Paul's first journey but suddenly left and returned to Jerusalem (Acts 13:1–13). A bitter quarrel later developed between Paul and Barnabas over Mark's action (Acts 15:36–41), but later Mark and Paul were reconciled (cf. Col. 4:10–11; Philemon 24). Since most scholars regard Colossians and Philemon as written at Rome, these passages from Paul's letters would also associate Mark with Rome.

It is Peter's connection with Mark, however, that particularly locates Mark at Rome. One of the last statements in 1 Peter is "She who is in Babylon, elect together with you, greets you; and so does Mark my son" (1 Peter 5:13). Peter no doubt is using symbolic language in his greetings to the readers, Christians in several Roman provinces in northern Turkey. "She" probably refers to a Christian congregation. "Babylon" was a symbolic name in Christian circles for a secular power hostile to the church; several times in Revelation "Babylon" implies Rome. Mark was not Peter's physical father, so "son" probably suggests that Peter converted Mark and became his spiritual father. Peter's statement also implies that since Mark was known to the readers of 1 Peter, he may have done some missionary work in northern Turkey.

Peter's reference to Mark as his "son," even if the word means spiritual son, suggests that Mark was much younger than Peter.

That Mark is nowhere mentioned by name among Jesus' disciples and that Mark is a son of Mary both suggest that Mark may have been a teenager during the earthly ministry of Jesus and was thus too young to be one of the Twelve or the 70.

In this connection it is interesting to note an incident recorded only in Mark's gospel: "Now a certain young man followed Him, having a linen cloth thrown around his naked body. And the young men laid hold of him, and he left the linen cloth and fled from them naked" (14:51–52). Since there is no other apparent reason for including this incident from the time of Jesus' arrest, most students of Scripture deduce that Mark is referring to his own experience and thus giving a clue to the authorship of the gospel. It was an experience that the disciples had not witnessed, for we are told in the previous verse that they had fled (14:50); only the youth who later wrote the account had been the victim.

STUDY QUESTION 3

How do the following passages agree with the tradition that Mark's gospel is closely related to Peter's preaching: Mark 1:16; 16:7; 8:29; 1:29; 1:36; Acts 10:36–43?

Peter's Gospel

According to tradition, as noted above, Mark wrote what Peter preached. The internal clues in this gospel certainly substantiate the connection between Mark and Peter. Mark's gospel begins with the call of Peter (1:16); at the end there is the resurrected Christ sending a message to His disciples and to Peter (16:7). Peter's confession is one of the climactic points of the document (8:29). Peter's house is the center of Jesus' ministry at Capernaum (1:29). Mark refers to Jesus' followers as "Simon and those who were with Him" (1:36). Occasionally Mark records incidents that show Peter's failings (e.g., the rebuke of Peter, 8:3l–33) but plays down items to his credit (e.g., the promise of the "keys")—which is understandable if the information came from Peter himself.

Pointing to the same conclusion is the parallel structure that is seen when we compare Mark's gospel with the sermon of Peter in the house of Cornelius in Acts 10:36–43. These eight verses of Acts parallel the geography and theology of Mark's gospel. In both, the geography proceeds from the baptism of John to Jesus' ministry in Galilee and on to His death and resurrection in Jerusalem. In both, the basic theology centers on the forgiveness of sins and on Jesus as Judge of the living and the dead.

STUDY QUESTION 4

What do the following passages indicate concerning the type of reader Mark had in mind?

A. Mark 3:17; 5:41; 7:34; 15:22, 34.

B. Mark 7:3–4; 14:12; 15:42.

Gentile Readers

The early tradition of the church, which associates Mark's gospel with Rome and Italy, agrees with the internal evidence that Mark wrote for Gentile readers. Mark cites the Old Testament only once (1:2–3) in contrast to the numerous quotations from the Old Testament in Matthew. In Mark, Hebrew and Aramaic expressions are explained: *"Boanerges*, that is, 'Sons of Thunder' " (3:17). *Talitha, cumi* is translated "Little girl, I say to you, arise" (5:41). *Ephphatha* means "Be opened" (7:34). *Golgotha* is translated "skull" (15:22). *Eloi, Eloi, lama sabachthani?* is rendered "My God, My God, why have You forsaken Me?" (15:34). Mark also includes explanations of Jewish practice—explanations that would be superfluous for Jewish readers: an explanation of what eating bread with defiled hands means (7:3–4); an explanation that Passover lambs were slaughtered on the first day of Unleavened Bread (14:12); an explanation that Preparation Day was the day before the Sabbath (15:42).

Pointing also to the conclusion that Mark had Gentile readers in mind is his distinct preference for Latin technical terms: *Praetorium* as an explanation for the Greek word for courtyard (15:16); *speculator* is transliterated from Latin into Greek for "executioner" (6:27); and the Latin *centurion* is transliterated into Greek letters (15:39, 44), while Matthew uses the Greek word for "ruler of a hundred" (8:5). Also pertinent is Mark's relation of Greek money to Roman currency: *lepta* is explained in terms of the Roman *quad-*

rans (12:42)—an important point since the *quadrans* apparently did circulate as a coin in the eastern Mediterranean countries.

Noteworthy also is Mark's reference to the four watches of the night (6:48; 13:35) in agreement with the Roman reckoning of time, although three watches of the night were traditional among the Jews. Some scholars see such a time pattern in Mark's account of Jesus' Passion: Jesus enters Jerusalem to share the Passover *in the evening* (14:17); His betrayal probably occurs at *midnight* (14:41); Peter denies Him when *the rooster crowed* (14:72); and He is brought before Pilate in early *morning* (15:1). If this structure was Mark's intention, the significance would be appreciated at Rome.

Agreeing with the external and other internal evidence that Mark wrote his gospel at Rome on the basis of Peter's preaching is Mark's candor—"calling a spade a spade" without any attempt to cast a halo around Jesus' followers—a characteristic one would expect from Peter, a man of action both with the sword and in the race to the tomb. Examples of Mark's candor are the portrayal of the lack of understanding of Jesus' disciples on many occasions (4:13; 6:52; 8:17, 21; 10:32) and the candid report of the attitude of Jesus' relatives, who considered Him to be "out of His mind" (3:21). All this evidence agrees, furthermore, with the numerous details included in Mark's gospel—details that could have come from an eyewitness such as Peter: wild beasts with Jesus in the wilderness (1:13); the presence of hired servants in Zebedee's boat (1:20); Andrew's living with Simon (1:29).

Situation at Rome

The tradition of the early church that Mark wrote for Christians in Rome and Italy fits the historical situation of these Christians in the middle sixties. A disastrous fire swept through Rome in A.D. 64. Only four of the fourteen wards of the city escaped. Rumors arose that Nero, the Roman emperor, had caused the fire. Although such rumors were no doubt unfounded, Nero was looking for a scapegoat. His Jewish wife, Poppaea Sabina, may have suggested that the blame be placed on the Christians, who already were unpopular among the Romans. Since they refused to represent God by means of a statue since of the First Commandment, some Romans regarded them as atheists. Because they ate the body and drank the blood of their Lord in Holy Communion, they were accused of cannibalism.

Under Nero, therefore, a dire persecution erupted against the Christians in Rome and parts of Italy. A Roman historian described the situation as follows:

> Nero fabricated scapegoats—and punished with every refinement the notoriously depraved Christians (as they were popularly called) . . . . First, Nero had self-acknowledged Christians arrested. Then, on their information, large numbers of others were condemned—not so much for incendiarism as for their antisocial tendencies. Their deaths were made farcical. Dressed in wild animals' skins, they were torn to pieces by dogs or crucified or made into torches to be ignited after dark as substitutes for daylight. (Tacitus, *Annals* 15. 44)

This situation forced the Christians literally to go underground—to the catacombs, a series of tunnels and tomb chambers cut in the soft rock—for the confessing of Christ could, and did, result in a martyr's death.

STUDY QUESTION 5

Clues that may associate Mark's gospel with comfort and encouragement for the Christians persecuted under Nero:

A. Note Mark 1:13; 3:19–30; 15:15–20.
B. Note Mark 9:49; 10:30; 13:9–13; 16:7.
C. Note Mark 1:25, 34; 1:44; 3:1–12; 5:43; 7:36; 8:30.

Comfort and Encouragement

The mass arrests and capital punishment probably continued for a brief time in and around Rome. Yet the Christians there had been exposed to martyrdom, which could occur again at any time. In his account of Peter's preaching at Rome, therefore, Mark seems to stress certain items in the ministry of Jesus that might parallel the experiences of the Roman Christians. Realizing that frightened men and women need encouragement and comfort, Mark wove into his gospel a pastoral response to the situation at Rome. He shows that a Christian can suffer no form of abuse that Jesus had not endured already. Certain details should take on added significance.

Only Mark, for example, mentions the presence of wild beasts with Jesus in the wilderness (1:13). Christians in Rome also had been in the wilderness of the catacombs and in the presence of wild beasts in the arena. Jesus had been falsely labeled as deranged by His family and as demonic by Jerusalem officials (3:21–30); Christians at Rome had been falsely labeled and misrepresented by Roman pagans. The betrayal of Jesus by one of His close associates (3:19) could give comfort and encouragement to those Roman Christians who were condemned on the basis of information given by others. Those followers at Rome who were scourged, tried before Roman magistrates, and condemned to death could readily recall the parallel experiences of their Savior (15:15–20).

Several of Jesus' statements could take on added significance for Roman readers: "For everyone will be seasoned with fire" (9:49). Jesus' promise of reward to those who follow Him includes the phrase "with persecutions" (10:30). Jesus warned that His followers would be beaten and would stand before rulers and kings as witnesses to the truth, that brother would betray brother to death, the father his child, children their parents, and that His followers would be hated because they belong to Him (13:9–13). The message of the risen Christ that His disciples *and Peter* should meet Him in Galilee (16:7) could extend special comfort and assurance of forgiveness to those at Rome who had denied before Roman magistrates that they were Christians.

The details of Mark's gospel are full of special meaning for people who were persecuted because they were Christians. They should not reject suffering and death, for their Lord had submitted to both. Jesus' resurrection showed that suffering and death were not the end for His followers, for Jesus would meet them again as he rejoined the disciples in Galilee. No Roman official has the final word—only God, who raises the dead and who will display His glory through the people who remain faithful to Him.

Secrecy in Mark

Another element in Mark's gospel that could have some relevance to the historical situation in Rome is Jesus' insistence on secrecy and silence concerning His identity. Jesus' identity as God's Son is stated in the first verse, confirmed by the Father both at Jesus' baptism (1:11) and at His transfiguration (9:7), declared by demons (1:24; 3:11; 5:7), and confessed by Peter (8:29) and by the Roman centurion (15:39), but it is expressed clearly by Jesus Himself only toward the end of the gospel (14:61–62). Throughout the document Mark presents Jesus as insisting that His identity not be revealed. Demons are not to reveal it (1:25, 34; 3:12), nor are those whom He healed (1:44; 5:43; 7:36), and the disciples are not to reveal Peter's confession to others (8:30). Of course there are other reasons for Mark's identification of Jesus as Son of Man in preference to Son of God, but it may not be too farfetched to see also a relevance to the situation in Rome. The secret existence in the catacombs, brought on by the danger of persecution and death, had a precedent in the life of Jesus, who also practiced secrecy in His early ministry concerning His identity as God's Son lest His mission be misinterpreted by those who were expecting a political leader to rescue the Jews from control by the Romans.

Theological Theme

At the beginning of the chapter we noted that Mark's first verse presents a clue to the structure of his gospel: Jesus is the Christ and the Son of God. Therefore he divides his document into two parts. The first part, describing Jesus' ministry in Galilee, reaches a climactic point in Peter's confession that Jesus is the Christ (8:29). The second part, concentrating on Jesus in Judea and Jerusalem, reaches another climactic point in the confession of the Roman soldier that Jesus is the Son of God (15:39). It is pertinent to note how Mark develops these two aspects of his theological theme.

Jesus as Christ

Mark prepares for Peter's confession by presenting Jesus as powerful in word and deed and challenging in His claims. Jesus' words are a source of amazement. "They were astonished at His teaching, for He taught them as one having authority, and not as the scribes" (1:22). "They were all amazed, so that they questioned among themselves, saying, 'What is this? What new doctrine is this?' " (1:27). "When the Sabbath had come, He began to teach in the synagogue. And many hearing Him were astonished, saying, 'Where did this Man get these things? And what wisdom is this which is given to Him?' " (6:2).

Jesus' deeds also were a cause for amazement. He manifested power over evil spirits (1:26, 34, 39; 5:13; 7:30). He cured sickness and infirmities—Peter's mother-in-law (1:30–31), a leper (1:42), a paralytic (2:3–12), a man with a withered hand (3:3–5), people with diseases (3:10), a woman with a hemorrhage (5:29), some sick people (6:5), a deaf mute (7:32–35), a blind man (8:23–25).

Jesus raised the dead (5:41–42), calmed the boisterous waves (4:39; 6:48–51), and gave a new desert bread (6:41–44; 8:6–9).

Jesus' claims presented another challenge—as forgiver of sins (2:10–11), as Lord of the Sabbath (2:28; 3:4), and as the reformer of Jewish traditions (7:1–23).

Reactions in Mark 1–8

The reactions to Jesus' astonishing words, deeds, and claims—the reaction to the central question of Mark 1–8, "Who then is this Jesus?" (cf. 4:41)—are varied. Jewish authorities such as priests, scribes, and Pharisees reject Him (2:6–7; 2:16–3:6; 7:5; 8:11). So do His own people and fellow townsmen (3:21; 6:2–4). Some of the common people, however, are more receptive, such as the Jews of Capernaum (1:22, 27–28), the leper (1:40), the paralytic and his friends (2:5), some bystanders (2:12), Levi (2:14), people of the Decapolis or Greek district of 10 cities (5:20), the woman sick for 12 years (5:28–34), the Syro-Phoenician woman (7:28), and the crowd that witnessed the cure of the deaf mute (7:37). Jesus' disciples show some indecision (4:41; 5:42; 6:51), and Mark presents them as slow learners (4:13; 6:52; 7:18; 8:17–21).

Only after this rapid presentation of Jesus' words, deeds, and claims, interspersed with positive, negative, and ambiguous reactions, does Jesus ask His chosen disciples point blank, "But who do you say that I am?" and receives Peter's answer, "You are the Christ" (8:29). So Peter's confession marks a climactic point in the theological theme of Mark's gospel and is a big step toward the answer to the question, "Who then is this Jesus?" He is the Christ.

STUDY QUESTION 6

Mark's description of Jesus as the Messiah (Christ):

A. Compare these passages with Daniel 7:13–14: Mark 8:38; 13:26; 14:62.

B. Compare with Isaiah 53 (and 52:13) these passages: Mark 9:9, 12, 31; 10:33–34, 45; 14:21, 41.

What Kind of Christ?

In the second part of his gospel Mark is intent on two things: (1) He moves the account in the direction of Jerusalem and Calvary.

(2) He develops a clarification of Jesus as the Christ—what kind of Christ is Jesus of Nazareth? The name Christ had misleading implications at the time of Jesus. It could mean savior, king, ruler, or deliverer, any of which ideas could be misunderstood when applied to Jesus. Mark, therefore, elaborates on his theological theme in the second part of his gospel by presenting Jesus Christ in terms of two predictions from the Old Testament, one by Daniel and the other by Isaiah.

The Old Testament book of Daniel (7:13-14) describes the coming of "One like the Son of Man" to whom will be given dominion and glory and kingdom, so that all peoples will serve Him and His dominion will last forever. Isaiah 53 contains the well-known prediction of Christ as a Suffering Servant, who is delivered up and lays down His life for the sins of many. It is interesting to note that the occurrences of the term "Son of Man" in the second part of Mark's gospel refer to these two Old Testament figures.

Three passages in Mark relate to Daniel's description of the final judgment scene: "Of him the Son of Man also will be ashamed when He comes in the glory of His Father with the holy angels" (8:38). "Then they will see the Son of Man coming in the clouds with great power and glory" (13:26). "You will see the Son of Man sitting at the right hand of the Power, and coming with the clouds of heaven" (14:62). There is another reference to the Son of Man in the early chapters of Mark: "Therefore the Son of Man is also Lord of the Sabbath" (2:28), which could refer to the possession of complete dominion described in Daniel 7:14.

The references to Jesus Christ in terms of Isaiah's Suffering Servant also are conspicuous. These references appear after Peter's confession (8:29): "He commanded them that they should tell no one the things they had seen, till the Son of Man had risen from the dead" (9:9; cf. Is. 52:13). "How is it written concerning the Son of Man, that He must suffer many things and be treated with contempt?" (9:12). "The Son of Man is being delivered into the hands of men, and they will kill Him. And after He is killed, He will rise the third day" (9:31). "The Son of Man will be delivered to the chief priests and to the scribes, and they will condemn Him to death and deliver Him to the Gentiles; and they will mock Him, and scourge Him, and spit on Him, and kill Him. And the third day He will rise again" (10:33–34). "The Son of Man did not come to be served, but to serve, and to give His life a ransom for many" (10:45). "The Son of Man indeed goes just as it is written of Him, but woe to that man by whom the Son of Man is betrayed!" (14:21).

"The Son of Man is being betrayed into the hands of sinners" (14:41).

These numerous references in the second part of the document indicate that Mark is becoming more specific about the identity of Jesus Christ. What kind of Christ is Jesus? He is a combination of Daniel's "One like the Son of Man" and Isaiah's Suffering Servant. The theological theme of the Suffering Servant, which Mark applies most appropriately to Jesus Christ, may also extend to the followers of Christ. On three occasions Mark has Jesus teaching His disciples that they too must take up the cross and become servants (8:34–35; 9:35; 10:42–44).

Suffering and sometimes death for Christ's cause, as we have noted above, was the lot of many Christians in Rome and Italy. Mark, therefore, seems to be encouraging his readers to take heart in their situation as suffering servants. They are following the example of their Lord and of His original disciples. They have hope, in spite of the present tribulations, for as Jesus passed through the cross to glory, so too will those who take up their cross and follow Him. For He is Jesus, Son of God, as Mark states both at the beginning of his gospel and at the end in the confession of the Roman centurion (1:1; 15:39).

Mark's Ending

A final brief comment may be made concerning the ending of Mark's gospel. According to the evidence of early manuscripts (Vaticanus and Sinaiticus) the last 12 verses (16:9–29) are not a part of the original manuscript. Other reasons for doubting the integrity of these verses may also be mentioned. Their style in Greek is different from the rest of Mark. The narrative of 16:9–20 does not continue that of 16:1–8—Mary Magdalene, for example, is introduced at 16:9, although she is mentioned at 16:1. In fact, 16:9–20 seems to be a summary of the appearances of Jesus recorded in Matthew, Luke, and John. Finally, some expressions occur in 16:9–20 that are not found elsewhere in the Gospel—Jesus is called Lord, for example, in 16:19, 20, but nowhere else does Mark use this title.

How Mark originally ended his gospel is a relatively minor matter and does not affect in the least the comments and interpretation sketched above. It is also possible that Mark may have died or been martyred before he completed the document.

Outline

    I. Theme or Title (1:1)

    II. Introduction: John, the Forerunner of Jesus (1:2–13)

    III. Galilean Period (1:14–9:50)

        A. Around the Sea of Galilee (1:14–5:43)

        B. In Galilee (6:1–9:50); note 8:29, Peter's Confession (a Jew and disciple)

    IV. Judean Period (10:1–16:8)

        A. Pre-Passion (10:1–13:37)

        B. Passion and Resurrection (14:1–16:8); note 15:39, the Centurion's Confession (a Gentile and Roman official)

4. Luke: Jesus for All Humanity

STUDY QUESTION 1

Luke has several features not contained in the other gospels. One of these is found in Luke 1:46–2:32, another in Luke 2:1–2 and 3:1. What do these distinctive features tell us about Luke? Three other distinctive inclusions are in Luke 2:41–52; 9:51–18:14; 24:50–53. What are they?

Luke is the fullest and most comprehensive of our four gospels. It is the longest document in the New Testament and includes several features that the other gospels do not have: (1) references to dates in secular history (2:1–2; 3:1); (2) Jesus at age 12 (2:41–53); (3) the four canticles (Magnificat, Benedictus, Gloria in Excelsis, Nunc Dimittis—1:46–2:32); (4) Jesus' travel account (9:51–18:14); and (5) the ascension of Jesus (24:50–53). In fact, the Third Gospel is only the first part of a two-volume publication that comprises Luke's gospel and the Acts of the Apostles. Together these two books constitute over one quarter of the entire New Testament (about 28 percent).

STUDY QUESTION 2

It is important to note that Luke and Acts are really two volumes of the same document.

A. Compare Luke 1:1–4 with Acts 1:1–5.

B. Note how the last chapter of Luke (24:33–52) ties in with the beginning of Acts (1:3–12).

Two Volumes

It is important to note at the beginning of this chapter that Luke and Acts originally formed one document written on two scrolls. Luke's account, therefore, begins with the birth of our Savior and continues through the expansion of God's Good News from Jerusalem to Rome. Our study of the identity of the author, his purpose, and the place and time of composition must take into consideration any clues given in both of these volumes. The intimate connection between Luke and Acts becomes clear from two areas: (1) the relationship between the ending of the gospel and the beginning of Acts; (2) the striking parallels in structure and detail in the two books.

The skillful way Luke has tied the conclusion of the gospel to the first chapter of Acts is impressive.

Luke		Acts
24:33–34, 36	Jesus appears to His apostles	1:3
24:36–43	Jesus proves His identity	1:3
24:49	Jesus' charge to His followers	1:4
24:47–48	Apostles as witnesses in Jerusalem	1:8
24:51–52	Apostles depart for Jerusalem	1:12

Even more impressive are the parallels in structure and detail between Luke and Acts.

Luke		Acts
1:1–4	Preface to Theophilus	1:1–2
3:22	Spirit descends in physical form	2:1–13
4:16–30	Inaugural sermon	2:14–40
5:17–26	Lame man healed	3:1–10
7:1–10	Centurion requests Jesus/Peter to come to his home	10:1–23
7:11–17	Widow and resurrection	9:36–43

9:51–19:28	Passion journey to Jerusalem	19:21–21:17
22:54	Jesus/Paul seized	21:30
22:63–64	Jesus/Paul slapped	23:2
22:66; 23:1, 8, 13	Four trials of Jesus/Paul	23–26
23:4, 14, 22	Jesus/Paul declared innocent three times	23:29; 25:25; 26:31

It is also clear that while Luke's gospel describes what "Jesus began both to do and teach" (Acts 1:1) from Galilee to Jerusalem, Acts continues to depict what the Holy Spirit continued to do through the early church in spreading the message of salvation from Jerusalem to Rome. Such parallelism in structure and details leads some scholars to conclude that Luke first outlined each volume and then fitted in the details. The parallelism certainly points to a single author for both parts of a two-volume work. Although the two volumes are separated in our Bibles (one grouped with the other gospels, and Acts placed before Paul's letters), we must keep in mind that Luke and Acts cannot be separated in our study of either volume.

STUDY QUESTION 3

One emphasis of Luke is that neither Jesus nor Christianity was politically subversive.

A. *Note Luke 23:6–12; 23:4, 14–15, 22; 23:41; 23:47.*
B. *Note Acts 13:6–12; 28:7–10; 16:38–39; 18:12–17; 23:29; 24:22–27; 25:24–27; 26:32; 28:30–31.*

The Gospel and the Roman World

We have mentioned that one exclusive feature of Luke's gospel is that he ties in various secular dates from the Roman world. Usually this feature evokes the comment that Luke is the historian among our evangelists. It is true that if Luke had not connected the birth of Jesus (2:1–2) and the beginning of the ministry of John the Baptist (3:1) with rulers in the Roman world, we could not be as informed about the probable dates of Jesus' birth and death. But there is more to this feature of Luke. He is aware of the secular Roman world and of the importance of Rome's attitude toward the budding Christian church. Since the days of Julius Caesar, the Roman government had granted favors to Jewish settlements in the Roman empire. What would be Rome's attitude toward the Christians, who experienced extensive persecution from Jewish settlements?

First, let us note the references to Roman emperors. The decree for the census was issued by Octavian, later known as Caesar Augustus (Luke 2:1–7). John the Baptist began his ministry in the 15th year of the reign of Octavian's successor, Tiberius Caesar (Luke 3:1). A famine took place in Judea when Claudius was emperor (Acts 11:28). The same ruler banished Jews from the city of Rome (Acts 18:2). Paul as a Roman citizen appealed to the Caesar known as Nero (Acts 25:11, 12, 25; 26:32; 27:24). In other words, the only Roman emperor of this period to whom Luke does not refer is Caligula, a "madman" who ruled for a very short time (A.D. 37–41).

Certainly Luke is not merely a name-dropper. He is a careful historian, connecting events of Christianity with secular dates and rulers. But is Luke more than a historian? Do the clues give any basis for regarding Luke as an apologist, a defender of the faith? Some say that one emphasis of Luke is to show that Christianity was not a subversive sect. That is, Luke is basically defending the early Christian movement from the claim that being a Christian was incompatible with being a good citizen, at a time when some officials were looking with suspicion on the Christian movement.

Along this line of thought we may note certain clues in Luke's gospel that emphasize strongly the innocence of Jesus, the founder of the Christian movement. While Matthew and Mark refer to Jesus' hearing before the Sanhedrin and his trial before Pilate, only Luke includes Jesus' appearance before Herod Antipas, the ruler of Galilee (23:6–12). That is, Luke suggests the agreement of Pilate, a Roman official, and Herod, a Jewish official, on the innocence of Jesus. In fact, Luke has Pilate pronouncing Jesus innocent three times (23:4, 14–15, 22). Luke mentions the innocence of Jesus also while He is on the cross. One of the criminals crucified with Jesus declares: "This Man has done nothing wrong" (23:41). The Roman centurion in Matthew (27:54) and Mark (15:39) recognizes Jesus as the Son of God, but Luke records the additional information that the centurion praised God and said: "Certainly this was a righteous Man!" (23:47). Luke considers it important that he underscore the innocence of Jesus, although He had been condemned to death by a Roman court of law and crucified as a common criminal. The innocence of Jesus would be an important point to make to anyone investigating Christianity as a possible threat to the Roman political regime.

As Luke stresses the innocence of Jesus in the gospel, so in Acts he continues to emphasize the political innocence of the Christian movement. He traces the expansion of early Christianity from Jerusalem through Judea, Samaria, Caesarea, Antioch of Syria, the Roman provinces in Asia Minor (Turkey today), Macedonia and Achaia in Greece, and ultimately to Rome, the capital of the empire. He often stresses the response of Roman officials to the Christian message. Two of these officials—one toward the beginning of Paul's first journey and one shortly before Paul reached Rome—are favorably impressed by Paul's message: Sergius Paulus on the island of Cyprus was converted (Acts 13:6–12), and Publius on the island of Malta, if not converted, at least presented gifts to Paul (Acts 28:7–10). Between these two incidents, Paul's message about Christ is brought to the attention of numerous officials, both local and Roman. Each time Paul is exonerated with the added implication that the Christian movement is politically innocent. These incidents include Paul's release by the magistrates of Philippi (Acts 16:35–39); his discharge before Gallio, the Roman governor of Achaia (Acts 18:12–17); and the admission of two Roman governors, Felix and Festus, that Paul had been unjustly accused in Jerusalem and Caesarea (Acts 23:29; 24:22–27; 25:24–27; 26:32). The final scene in Acts (28:30–31)—Paul under house arrest in Rome with freedom to teach and preach without hindrance—pictures Rome as seeing no conflict between its political policies and the Christian movement. The general effect of these clues is that, while Luke certainly has other purposes in mind, he is attempting also to answer the charge that a Christian could not serve both Christ and the Roman government.

Luke 1:1–4

In this connection some remarks about the prolog to Luke's gospel are in place. An analysis of these introductory verses presents several points of interest. The disciples of Jesus, not remaining silent, had handed down the essential facts of the Gospel message. Some had developed narratives of Jesus' ministry—no doubt oral and written. That the written accounts include the gospels of Matthew and Mark is a possibility, although not a certainty. Luke resolved to compose his two-volume document on the basis of careful research—with suitable time and sources available during Paul's imprisonments at Caesarea for two years, followed by another two-year house arrest at Rome. Luke's two volumes had the expressed intent of making a certain "most excellent" Theophilus acquainted with the truth of what he had been "informed."

The two expressions that we have placed in quotation marks deserve special comment, for the possible identity of Theophilus depends so much on their interpretation. The Greek word rendered "informed" has two meanings: "instructed" or "informed." If the former is the more correct translation in Luke's prolog, the deduction would be that Theophilus is a recent convert to Christianity and that Luke is composing this lengthy two-volume document for the catechetical instruction of one particular recent convert (and perhaps a few other recent converts). Should "informed" be the proper translation, a much broader purpose may be attributed to Luke—namely, that Theophilus is a Roman magistrate who needs additional knowledge about the Christian movement to carry out some official function. That Luke used the Greek word in the sense of "inform" rather than "instruct" is clear from its occurrence in two passages in Acts (21:21, 24).

The other important word, rendered "most excellent," also merits comment. This word occurs only three other times in the New Testament. Each time it is used in Acts. Twice it is a title for Felix (23:26; 24:3), and once it is a title for Festus (26:25). That is, in each of these three occurrences the word "most excellent" refers to a Roman magistrate. This fact seems to lean in favor of also regarding Theophilus as a Roman magistrate and of interpreting the other Greek word as "informed" rather than "instructed." Therefore Theophilus need not be a Christian convert who is to be instructed in the Christian message; he could just as well be a Roman magistrate whom Luke addresses for a more general purpose—the purpose suggested above—to portray the Christian movement as politically harmless to Rome.

STUDY QUESTION 4

Luke includes several incidental clues to the nationality of his readers.

A. Compare Luke 23:33 with Matthew 27:33; Mark 15:22; John 19:17.
B. Note Luke 1:26; 4:31; 8:26; 22:1; 23:50; 24:13.

Gentile Readers

Theophilus is a Gentile name, meaning "friend of God." It is pertinent, therefore, to examine any clues in Luke's gospel that might point to Luke's writing for Gentiles rather than for Jews. We might note that Luke avoids the Jewish address "rabbi," which may be puzzling to non-Jewish readers, although the term is used in Matthew, Mark, and John. Luke also omits the Jewish "hosanna" from the account of Jesus' triumphal entry into Jerusalem (19:28–40), although both Matthew and Mark use the term. Referring to the place of Jesus' crucifixion, Luke uses only the Greek word for skull, *kranion* (23:33), while Matthew (27:33), Mark (15:22), and John (19:17) also call the place by its Hebrew name Golgotha. Luke takes the trouble to explain Jewish localities and customs— he refers to both Nazareth and Capernaum as cities of Galilee (1:26; 4:31); he mentions the country of the Gadarenes or Gerasenes, "which is opposite Galilee" (8:26); he speaks of the feast of Unleavened Bread, "which is called Passover" (22:1); he identifies Arimathea as "a city of the Jews" (23:51); and he specifies that Emmaus was "about seven miles from Jerusalem" (24:13). Finally, Luke's gospel contains only a few of Jesus' criticisms of the scribes and Pharisees, indicating a circle of readers not particularly interested in questions of first-century Judaism.

STUDY QUESTION 5

Evidence for the identity of Luke as the author of Luke-Acts.

A. Note the "we" passages: Acts 16:11–17; 20:5–21:18; 27:1–28:16. Whom do these passages eliminate as the author?
B. Note Col. 4:14; Luke 4:38; 5:12. Compare Luke 8:43 with Mark 5:26.
C. Note Col. 4:10–14; Acts 1:19; 28:2–4. Compare 2 Cor. 8:16–19 and Gal. 2:3.

Author

So far we have been referring to the author of the Third Gospel (and of Acts) as Luke, since he has been so identified in the tradition of the early church. Now we should examine briefly the evidence for the identification. In the second volume, which we now call Acts, there are three passages that contain the pronoun "we" frequently. These verses indicate that the author includes himself in the company of St. Paul. The three passages are (1) Acts 16:11–17, Paul's trip from Troas to Philippi on his second journey; (2) Acts 20:5–21:18, Paul's return on his third journey from Philippi to Jerusalem; and (3) Acts 27:1–28:16, Paul's trip from Caesarea to Rome.

Granted that these three passages identify the author as one of Paul's companions, the next question is, Which companion? Paul had numerous companions. When we read the verse (Acts 20:4) before the beginning of the second "we" passage (Acts 20:5–6), we see that several of Paul's companions are eliminated as the author. Sopater, Aristarchus, Secundus, Gaius, Timothy, Tychicus, and Trophimus are distinguished from the "we"; the author must be some other of Paul's companions. Continuing the process of elimination, the author could not be Barnabas, who accompanied Paul on his first journey, for then a "we" passage would be expected to begin in Acts 13–14, which relate Paul's first journey. The same reasoning would exclude Silas (or Silvanus), who accompanied Paul from the beginning of the second journey, for then a "we" passage would be expected to begin with Acts 15:23 and continuing until 17:14. Likewise, if Timothy had been the author, a "we" section would extend from Acts 16:4 to 17:9.

Who then remains of Paul's companions as the probable author of Luke-Acts? According to Paul's epistles the only important friends of Paul not yet eliminated are Titus and Luke. But wait a moment. Titus also is eliminated by Galatians 2:1, which tells of a visit by Paul to Jerusalem with Titus. This visit is related either in Acts 11 or in Acts 15, and neither chapter contains a "we" section, so that takes care of Titus as a possible author. The result is that by the process of elimination the evidence from the New Testament points to Luke as the author of our two-volume document Luke-Acts, agreeing with the tradition of the early church.

Luke in the New Testament

There are three definite references to Luke in the New Testament, assuming that Lucius in Romans 16:21 and Acts 13:1 designates a different person. The three references are (1) Col. 4:14, which refers to him as the beloved physician; (2) Philemon 24, which calls him one of Paul's fellow workers; and (3) 2 Tim. 4:11, which states that Luke is with Paul during an imprisonment, no doubt at Rome.

That Luke was a physician seems to be true on the basis of the clues in his gospel. Some scholars see numerous medical terms in his writings, while other specialists point out that any educated man of that day would be acquainted with some medical terminology, as is the case in the 20th century. The fact remains, however, that Luke describes illnesses and ailments with more medical precision than we find in the other gospel accounts. Peter's mother-in-law, for example, suffers from "a high fever" (4:38), and a leper is described as "full of leprosy" (5:12). But more significant is the case of a woman suffering from a hemorrhage. Luke (in the Greek text) omits the comment that she had spent her savings on doctors without being cured (8:43; cf. Mark 5:26). Luke the physician refuses to disparage fellow physicians.

The reference to Luke in Colossians is also a clue that Luke was a Gentile. In the previous verses (Col. 4:10–11) Paul mentions Aristarchus, Mark, Barnabas, and Justus as "my only fellow workers . . . who are of the circumcision"—that is, Paul identifies these people as Jews. Then in the following verses (Col. 4:12–14) Paul lists three more names—Epaphras, Luke, and Demas—implying that these three were not "of the circumcision" but were Gentiles.

Two passages in Acts corroborate the clue given in Colossians. In referring to the plot of ground bought with the money paid to Judas, Luke writes: "That field is called in their own language, Akel Dama, that is, Field of Blood" (Acts 1:19). Note that the Jewish name Akel Dama is a word in *their own* language. That is, Luke is distinguishing his race from that of the Jews. The same implication is also present in the last chapter of Acts (28:2–4). Luke describes the inhabitants of Malta, where Paul experienced shipwreck, as "barbarians" in the Greek text, translated as "natives" in some English versions. The people at Malta were Phoenicians, a Semitic people and thus related to the Jews. It would be odd for a Jew to refer to the people of Malta as "barbarians." But it was customary for Greeks to refer to all non-Greeks as "barbarians," which basically meant merely "strangers" or "non-Greeks."

One other passage in the New Testament may be pertinent to the racial background of Luke, at least in the view of some scholars. In his Second Letter to the Corinthians (8:16–19) Paul speaks of

54

sending Titus to Corinth to expedite the collection for Jerusalem and adds: "We have sent with him the brother whose praise is in the gospel throughout all the churches." Some scholars believe that "the brother," which could also be translated "his brother," refers to Luke, who then would be the brother of Titus. That Titus was a Gentile is clear from Paul's statement in Gal. 2:3 that Titus was a Greek. This deduction would agree with a scribal addition to at least one ancient manuscript of Second Corinthians that this letter was written from Philippi, a city of Macedonia, and delivered by Titus and Luke. If this deduction is true, it would help explain why Titus and Luke are never mentioned in Acts, in spite of their important contribution to Paul's work as seen from his epistles—that is, the author Luke does not wish to glamorize the name or reputation of himself or that of his brother.

Luke's Sources

In the preface to his gospel, Luke (in the Greek text) speaks of "having investigated carefully all things from the beginning" (1:3). This statement raises the matter of Luke's sources. Where could he have received the information included in his two-volume work? He himself of course was an eyewitness to much of the information included in the second half of Acts. Paul would have been a primary source for Paul's missionary journeys. Other fellow workers of Paul, such as Silas, Timothy, and Aristarchus, would also be reliable sources of information. Concerning the early years of the church, information could be gleaned from Philip the evangelist and Mnason, an early disciple at Jerusalem, each of whom Luke visited with Paul at Caesarea and at Jerusalem (Acts 21:8, 15–16). During Paul's two-year imprisonment at Caesarea (Acts 24:27) Luke would have had time to travel through Palestine and interview various individuals for information, including Mark's mother and James the brother of the Lord. While Paul was under house arrest at Rome for two years, Luke would have had access to information from Peter and Mark (Acts 28:30; 1 Peter 5:13). In brief, numerous sources would have been available to Luke.

Time and Place

The previous section points to Paul's imprisonment at Caesarea and his house arrest at Rome, a period of four years, as the probable time and place for Luke's composition of Luke-Acts. Does this assumption agree with the evidence in his two-volume work?

To discuss this question we should especially consider some clues in Acts.

First, we may note that in Acts Luke makes no reference to certain events important to the church that occurred in the middle and end of the sixties. There is no mention of the Jewish War against Rome (A.D. 66–70) or of the fall of Jerusalem in A.D. 70. Nor does Luke refer to the persecution under Nero (about A.D. 64–65). Luke is also silent concerning the death of James, the Lord's brother (A.D. 62). Second, there is no mention of the outcome of Paul's trial in Rome—a decision that certainly would have interested the readers of Acts. Third, the theological issues in Acts are topics that confronted the early church particularly before A.D. 60—the Jewish-Gentile controversy and the food served at the feasts in the early church. Fourth, the attitude of the state toward the church certainly points to a time before the persecution under Nero. The final verse refers to Paul's preaching and teaching about "the Lord Jesus Christ with all confidence, no one forbidding him" (Acts 28:31). Does this statement present a picture of a situation before or after the Neronian persecution? Finally, one of the most important clues is that Acts shows no acquaintance with the letters of Paul. That is, Luke seems to have written Luke-Acts before Paul's epistles were generally circulated among the congregations of the early church. While these arguments may not be conclusive, they do show good reasons for dating Luke-Acts in the early sixties.

Outline

The general outline of Luke's gospel frequently is compared with the outline of Mark. In brief, Luke may be divided as follows:

    I. Preface (1:1–4)
   II. Beginnings: Infancy of John the Baptist and Jesus through the temptation of Jesus (1:5–4:13)
  III. Jesus' ministry in Galilee (4:14–9:50)
  IV. Journey from Galilee to Jerusalem (9:51–19:27)
   V. Jesus in Jerusalem through His passion, death, resurrection, and ascension (19:28–24:53)

We note that the basic outline of Luke agrees with the outline of Mark—a period in Galilee followed by a period in Judea. But Luke has two major insertions (plus additional material on Jesus' birth, passion, and resurrection): (1) Luke 6:20–8:3 is inserted between Mark 3:19 and 20, and (2) Luke 9:51–18:14, usually called the travel account, is inserted between Mark 9:50 and 10:1. Luke also omits the material covered by Mark 6:45–8:26.

This brief comparison between the outlines of Mark and Luke merits two observations. First, it seems that Luke was acquainted with Mark's gospel. Since we already have placed Mark's gospel in Rome in the late fifties or early sixties, this comparison of Luke with Mark supports the time and place for Luke's gospel discussed above. The second observation is that the long section in Luke that is not contained in Mark, usually called the travel account (9:51–18:14), may furnish us with our best clues to some of the characteristics of Luke's gospel.

STUDY QUESTION 6

Characteristics of Luke's gospel

A. *Note 15:2, 11–32; 18:9–14; 19:10; 22:31–34; 23:42–43.*

B. *Note 2:32; 3:4–6, 12–14, 23–38; 4:25–27; 9:52; 10:29–37; 17:11–19.*

C. *Note 1:15, 35; 3:22; 4:1, 14, 18; 10:21; 1:41–42, 67; 2:25–27; 3:16; 11:13; 12:11–12.*

D. *Note 3:21; 5:15–16; 6:12; 9:18–22, 29; 10:17–22; 22:39–46; 23:34, 46; 6:12; 11:5–13; 18:1–8, 9–14; 22:31–32; 22:40, 41–42; 23:34.*

Characteristics

One of the dominant characteristics of Luke's gospel is the stress on the completeness of God's grace through Jesus. The parables of the lost son (15:11–32) and of the Pharisee and the tax collector (18:9–14) underscore the free forgiveness through Christ in contrast to the piety of the Pharisees. Luke emphasizes that Jesus "receives sinners and eats with them" (15:2). Jesus furthermore intercedes for the disciple who will deny Him (22:31–34), promises Paradise to the criminal beside Him (23:42–43), and clearly states: "The Son of Man has come to seek and to save that which was lost" (19:10).

Another characteristic of Luke is the universality of God's grace through Jesus—that the Gospel message is meant for all people.

In contrast to Matthew, Luke traces Jesus' genealogy back to Adam, the father of all mankind (3:23–38). Gentile soldiers are baptized by John (3:12–14). There is great interest in Samaritans (9:52; 10:29–37; 17:11–19). The angel's message of good will is directed to all people (2:14). Simeon speaks of Jesus as a light for the Gentiles (2:32). In discussing John the Baptist, Luke continues the quotation from Isaiah to include the words, "all flesh shall see the salvation of God" (3:4–6). In Luke Jesus cites two illustrations from the Old Testament that concern non-Israelites: the widow of Zarephath and Naaman the Syrian (4:25–27).

Also dominant in Luke's gospel is an emphasis on the Holy Spirit. His influence is present in John the Baptist (1:15), in Mary (1:35), in Jesus (3:22; 4:1, 14, 18; 10:21), in Elizabeth (1:41–42), in Zacharias (1:67), and in Simeon (2:25–27). The Holy Spirit also is present in Baptism (3:16), is promised to the disciples (12:11–12), and is a gift that God will give "to those who ask Him" (11:13). The emphasis on the Holy Spirit in Luke's gospel continues in his second volume—but more on that under Acts.

An emphasis on prayer is another characteristic of Luke's gospel. He refers to nine prayers of Jesus, seven of which appear only in Luke. They are associated with important events in Jesus' ministry—His Baptism (3:21), a day of miracles (5:15–16), the choosing of the disciples (6:12), the first prediction of the passion (9:18–22), the transfiguration (9:29), the return of the 70 (10:17–22), teaching the disciples how to pray (11:1), Gethsemane (22:39–46), the cross (23:34, 46). On one occasion Jesus withdraws into a desert and spends an entire night in prayer (6:12). Three of the parables peculiar to Luke concern prayer—the friend at midnight (11:5–13), the unrighteous judge (18:1–8), and the Pharisee and the tax collector (18:9–14). Only Luke records that Jesus prayed for Peter (22:31–32), that in Gethsemane He encouraged the disciples to pray (22:40), and that He prayed for His enemies (23:34) and for Himself (22:41–42).

It is interesting to note that these four characteristics of Luke's gospel—the completeness of God's grace, the universality of God's grace, the emphasis on the Holy Spirit, and the emphasis on prayer—are also dominant in the writings of Paul. The apostle to the Gentiles stressed that salvation comes by God's grace alone without works, that this salvation is meant for all nations and races, that our faith is the gift of the Holy Spirit, and that prayer is one of the primary responses in the life of a Christian. These parallel emphases in both Luke and Paul point to what we might expect to result from their companionship and joint missionary work as described by Luke in Acts.

We may close this unit by merely listing other features present in Luke's gospel:

A focus on individuals (1:5–64; 10.38–42; 19:1–10; 23:39–43)

An interest in social outcasts (7:36–50; 19:8–10; 23:39–43)

A portrayal of women (7:11–17, 36–50; 10:38–42; 23:27–31)

An interest in children (7:12; 8:42; 9:38)

Social relationships (7:36–50; 11:37–44; 14:1–4; 19:1–10; 24:13–32)

Poverty and wealth (6:20, 30; 14:11–14; 16:14–15)

Joyfulness (1:14, 44, 47; 6:23; 15:23, 32)

It is small wonder that Luke's gospel has played such an influential role in the church, a gospel that begins and ends with rejoicing (1:14; 24:52), a feature also of the four canticles peculiar to Luke: Magnificat (1:46–55), Benedictus (1:68–79), Gloria in Excelsis (2:14), and Nunc Dimittis (2:29–32).

5. Acts: Gospel of God's Grace Spread to Rome

STUDY QUESTION 1

Comment on the suitability of the title to the content of the Acts of the Apostles. What hint does Acts 1:1– 8 give concerning the content of Acts?

Since the previous chapter on Luke's gospel discussed such topics as author, time and place, and readers, there is no need for repeating these in a study of Luke's second volume, generally known as the Acts of the Apostles. We may mention, however, that this title does not belong to the original document but was added after the two volumes became separated. Only when the first volume was placed with the other gospels was there a need for a separate title.

The title is not very accurate and could be misleading. Luke's second volume does not include the actions of many apostles— only Peter and Paul among the apostles are the main characters, with John and James mentioned incidentally. Other characters who are not apostles loom large in the volume—Stephen, Philip, Barnabas, and Agabus, for example. The title could be misleading, furthermore, by suggesting a narrative of human achievement or actions, when in fact the guiding force in the spread of Christianity from Jerusalem to Rome is rather the Holy Spirit, as is clear from Luke's account. The opening verse of Acts makes it clear that the previous volume, Luke's gospel, dealt with "all that *Jesus began* both to do and teach." The present volume will contain an account of what the exalted Christ *continues* to do and teach through the *early church* and its leaders under the guidance of the *Holy Spirit* promised previously by Jesus (1:1–8).

STUDY QUESTION 2

The importance of Acts.

A. Why is Acts important to the study of the early church?

B. Why is Acts important to the study of Paul's epistles?

Importance of Acts

The importance of Acts for our understanding of the early church cannot be exaggerated. It is our only continuous record of what developed in the first 30 years of Christianity. It does not give us a complete history, of course, for Luke's account is selective. But without Acts there would be a huge vacuum in our knowledge of the early church, as there is concerning the period after the time covered by Acts, e.g., from A.D. 60 to 90. Acts is also extremely important in understanding the background and chronology of Paul's letters. Without Acts there would be great gaps in our knowledge of the relationship between Paul and the origin of the churches to which he wrote. We also would be at a complete loss in arranging his letters in chronological order.

Acts is extremely important, furthermore, because it has been the focus of attention by many scholars who since the 19th century have taken a negative approach to the reliability of several documents in the New Testament—particularly by those critics who see certain discrepancies between the account in Acts and Paul's epistles. In brief, Acts has been the battleground for numerous attacks on Scripture. But we shall have more to say on this subject later.

Twofold Outline

Acts has been outlined in three different ways—twofold, threefold, and sixfold. Each outline may be supported by clues in the text. A twofold outline would be:

I. Petrine section (chapters 1–12)
II. Pauline section (chapters 13–28).

The primary evidence for such an outline is the parallelism between the two sections. Just as we noticed previously in discussing Luke's gospel that there are parallels in details and structure between Luke's gospel and Acts, so it is not difficult to observe parallels between the first part and the second part of Acts. Some of these, though not meant to be exhaustive, might be listed as follows:

Petrine section	Pauline section
healing of lame beggar (3:1–10)	healing of lame man at Lystra (14:8–11)
Peter and magic (8:14–25)	Paul and magic (13:4–12; 19:13–19)
raising of Tabitha/Dorcas (9:36–43)	reviving of Eutychus (20:7–12)
Peter in prison (4:1–22; 5:17–42)	Paul in prison (16:16–40)
Peter miraculously released from prison (12:7–11)	Paul miraculously released from prison (16:26–34)
Peter beaten at Jerusalem (6:40)	Paul beaten at Philippi (16:22–23)
attempt to worship Peter (10:25)	attempt to worship Paul (14:8–18)
stoning of Stephen (7:54–60)	stoning of Paul (14:19–20)
Peter addresses Jerusalem Council (15:7–11)	Paul addresses Jerusalem Council (15:12)
eunuch studying Scripture (8:26–40)	Bereans studying Scripture (17:10–12)
angel encourages apostles to continue preaching (5:17–21)	vision encourages Paul to continue preaching (18:9–11)
Peter observes Jewish ceremonies (3:1)	Paul observes Jewish ceremonies (18:18; 21:23–26)
Peter before Sanhedrin (4:5–22; 5:22–42)	Paul before Sanhedrin (22:30–23:10)
Peter heals ill people (5:15–16)	Paul heals ill people (28:8–9)
Peter strikes Ananias and Sapphira dead (5:1–10)	Paul blinds the magician Elymas (13:8–11)

Some scholars in the 19th century tried to deduce too much from a twofold outline with its parallels. They incorrectly assumed that the author (not Luke, but someone in the second century) wished to show how an early theology of Peter was harmonized with a later theology of Paul and developed into the beliefs of the Christian church. It is far better to see these parallels merely as a characteristic of Luke in Acts, just as he has a tendency toward parallelism of structure and details between the two volumes of his entire writing (Luke and Acts). Luke was probably influenced also by Paul's statement that he was to convert Gentiles while Peter converted Jews (Gal. 2:7–9). Luke thus depicted their activities in two parallel pictures in the two parts of Acts.

Threefold Outline

On the basis of Acts 1:8 many students of Scripture prefer to see a threefold division of Acts. In this verse Jesus says, "You shall receive power when the Holy Spirit has come upon you; and you shall be witnesses to Me in Jerusalem, and in all Judea and Samaria, and to the end of the earth." Although four places are mentioned—Jerusalem, Judea, Samaria, the end of the earth—the structure in the Greek text makes it clear that Judea and Samaria are to be understood together to denote one step in the advancement of the Gospel (two nouns with one article). In the English translation the prepositions likewise indicate a threefold division: "*in* Jerusalem, and *in* all Judea and Samaria, and *to* the end of the earth." Such an outline, based on Acts 1:8, would be:

I. Gospel in Jerusalem (chapters 1–7)
II. Gospel in Judea and Samaria (chapters 8–12)
III. Gospel to the end of the earth (chapters 13–28).

Since the phrase "the end of the earth" could be an expression referring to Rome, and since Acts depicts the advancement of the Gospel to Rome, a threefold outline has much to commend it.

Sixfold Outline

There is still another basis for making divisions within Acts, again based on internal clues. The clues are six summarizing statements (6:7; 9:31; 12:24; 16:5; 19:20; 28:31), each marking off a separate section and indicating a step in the spread of the Gospel from Jerusalem to Rome. An outline of Acts based on these six summarizing statements would be:

I. The Gospel grows *in Jerusalem* (1:1–6:7: "The *Word* of God spread, and the number of the disciples multiplied greatly in Jerusalem, and a great many of the priests were obedient to the faith.")
II. The Gospel triumphs *over persecution* and goes *to Samaria; Saul* (Paul) *is called* (6:8–9:31: "Then the *churches* throughout all Judea, Galilee, and Samaria had peace and were edified. And walking in the fear of the Lord and in the comfort of the Holy Spirit, they were multiplied.")

III. The Gospel becomes a *light to the Gentiles* as Peter converts Cornelius and the church is established at Antioch (9:32–12:24: "The *Word* of God grew and multiplied.")

IV. The Gospel *unites Jews and Gentiles* in one church as a result of Paul's first journey and the Apostolic Council (12:25–16:5: "The *churches* were strengthened in the faith, and increased in number daily.")

V. The Gospel advances *to Macedonia, Achaia, and Asia* as Paul makes his second and third journeys (16:6–19:20: "The *Word* of the Lord grew mightily and prevailed.")

VI. The Gospel is *witnessed before magistrates and authorities* (cf. Luke 12:11) and *also at Rome* (19:21–28:31: ". . . preaching the kingdom of God and teaching the things which concern the Lord Jesus Christ with all confidence, no one forbidding him.")

It is interesting to note that the first five summarizing statements alternate the stress on two key words, *Word* and *churches*, while the final one refers to the content of the Word that builds the church.

So there are three legitimate ways to outline Acts, each resting on certain clues in the text and each emphasizing a different aspect of Acts. Instead of attempting to rate these three outlines, it is better to note that all of them indicate the orderly arrangement of the document and the clear planning of the author.

STUDY QUESTION 4

Two of the basic themes in Acts are geographical and theological.

A. *What is the geographical theme, noting Acts 1:8 and the threefold and sixfold outlines?*

B. *What is the theological theme, noting the development from Acts 3:1 to 8:14 to 10:1–48 to 11:1–3 to 11:19–26 to 15:1–29?*

C. *Note that two separate questions are decided in Acts 15:1–29.*

D. *Note how Acts emphasizes the importance of two events (in chapters 10 and 11, and in chapters 9, 22, and 26).*

Two Basic Themes

Just as Acts has three possible intertwining outlines, so there are two intertwining themes basic to Acts. One is geographical; the other is theological. The geographical theme of Acts is clear from the second and third outlines presented above. Christianity begins as a movement confined to Jerusalem. It soon spreads through Judea and Samaria along the northern coast of the Mediterranean Sea. Finally it reaches Rome, the capital of the political empire of that day.

The theological theme of Acts is intertwined by Luke with the geographical theme. The church begins with Pentecost at Jerusalem, the center of the Jewish religion. After some internal problems and external opposition from the Jews, the church expands to include Samaritans, who were considered second-rate citizens by the Jews. Then some Gentiles are converted by Peter at the home of Cornelius. The importance of this fact is underlined by Luke through a repetition of the event in two successive chapters (10 and 11). Another important aspect of the spread of Christianity from Jews to Gentiles is the conversion of Saul, who later becomes an apostle to the Gentiles. Again Luke emphasizes the importance of Paul's conversion by the means of repetition, relating Paul's experience in one chapter (9) and retelling it twice in later chapters (22 and 26). At the conclusion of Acts the church has permeated the Gentile world, being established in various Roman provinces and finally reaching the capital of the Gentile Roman world.

The theological problems presented by the inclusion of Gentiles into an originally Jewish movement come to a climax in the center of the document—at the Council of Jerusalem in Acts 15. Two questions are basic to the theological theme of Jewish versus Gentile Christianity. One question concerns the admittance of Gentiles to the church. Must they submit to the Jewish ceremonial law in general and to the practice of circumcision in particular? The other question involves the unity of the church that now includes many Gentiles as a result of Paul's first journey. How is unity to be obtained, for example, at the love feasts if Gentiles insist on eating foods commonly considered unfit by Jews? The Council of Jerusalem settles these two questions. On the first question the validity of the Gospel is maintained by the refusal to insist on the circumcision of Gentiles. On the second question the unity of a Jewish-Gentile church is maintained by the request that Gentiles refrain from eating certain foods at the love feasts that might offend the Jews.

STUDY QUESTION 5

An appropriate title for Acts might be: "The Guidance of the Holy Spirit."

A. *Cite passages in Acts to substantiate such a title.*
B. *Note three occasions when the Holy Spirit gave special gifts: Acts 2:5–13; 8:1–24; 10:44–48. Why on these occasions?*

The Holy Spirit in Acts

Another basic theme in Acts is the activity and influence of the Holy Spirit. As noted above, the first eight verses in Acts imply that the Holy Spirit is to be the guiding force in continuing what Jesus began to do and teach in His ministry. This stress becomes clear as Luke elaborates on the function of the Holy Spirit throughout Acts. The disciples are to wait in Jerusalem for the Spirit's coming (1:4–5), as Jesus promised (1:8) and as happened 50 days later (2:1–39). Early missionaries receive instruction from the Holy Spirit: Philip (8:29), Peter (10:19–20; 11:12), leaders of Antioch (13:1–3), Agabus and Paul (21:10–11). The Holy Spirit empowers people to proclaim the Gospel: the apostles (2:4; 4:31), Peter (4:8), Stephen (6:10), Barnabas (11:22–24). Conversion occurs through the Holy Spirit: Pentecost (2:38), Paul (9:17–18), Cornelius (10:44–47; 11:15). The Holy Spirit empowers people to endure persecution: the apostles (4:29–31), Paul (9:16–17; 13:50–52). The Holy Spirit guides Paul in his missionary travels (13:2–4; 16:6–7; 20:22–23; 21:4, 11). In brief, Luke emphasizes that the leaders of the church are men of the Holy Spirit and that their decisions are guided by the Holy Spirit. An appropriate title to Luke's second volume might be "The Guidance of the Holy Spirit."

On three specific occasions the Holy Spirit empowers Christians with special gifts. Each of these three occasions is most important in the spread of the Gospel message. First, at Pentecost, when the church is established, the Holy Spirit sends the disciples the special gift to speak in foreign languages (2:5–13). Jews and proselytes (converts to Judaism) are present. Then when the Gospel message is shared with the Samaritans, who are considered second-rate citizens and not full-blooded Jews, the Holy Spirit again sends special gifts (8:4–25). Also at the home of Cornelius, the first Gentile convert, the Holy Spirit bestows special gifts (10:44–48). Thus it is the Holy Spirit who is the guiding influence in spreading Christianity first among Jews at Jerusalem, then among Samaritans, and finally among Gentiles.

STUDY QUESTION 6

The sermons of Peter and Paul in Acts contain similar topics. Summarize the content of the following sermons: Acts 2:14–39; 3:12–26; 13:16–41.

Early Preaching

Acts presents another basic element: the style and content of preaching in the early church. Early Christian preaching does not emphasize religious duties, moral standards, or a political reformation. It proclaims rather a person, Jesus, who was crucified, but who the Christians know is alive. It points to Old Testament prophecies that were fulfilled in Him. It stresses Jesus' life, death, and particularly His resurrection for the justification of His followers. It includes His ascension to God's right hand as Lord of the living and the dead. It reminds the people of Jesus' return in judgment and challenges them to repentance, faith, and Baptism. Various individuals proclaim the Gospel message in Acts, but Peter and Paul preach most frequently. When they proclaim the Gospel message, the details and examples vary, but the core of their message concentrates on Jesus, the crucified and risen Lord of the church.

There are, of course, variations of emphasis in the preaching of the early church. When addressing primarily Jews, deliverance from the law is stressed. In speaking to pagans, the sermon might include deliverance from the power of demons. To the Jew, Jesus is the promised Messiah. To the non-Jew, He is the Lord and conqueror of all forces of evil. But in spite of slight variations, the same basic Gospel is presented to all. It is a message that must be kept pure, not merged with elements of other beliefs present in the Roman world. Christianity, like Judaism, would have nothing to do with the practices of pagan religions.

STUDY QUESTION 7

Paul's three journeys.

A. List Paul's itinerary on the first journey in Acts 13–14.
B. List Paul's itinerary on the second journey in Acts 15:36–18:22.
C. List Paul's itinerary on the third journey in Acts 18:23–21:17.

Paul's Journeys

We mentioned above that Acts gives us a connected account of the spread of Christianity from Jerusalem to Rome, emphasizing in the latter half the journeys of Paul. Acts is extremely important, therefore, for understanding the background and chronological order of Paul's epistles. To prepare for later chapters, which will discuss Paul's letters, it will be helpful to get a "bird's eye view" of Paul's journeys, so that his epistles may fit into their proper place in Paul's career.

Acts details three missionary journeys of Paul. The first journey begins with Paul and Barnabas going with Mark from Antioch of Syria to the island of Cyprus and then to the Roman province of Pamphylia (southern Turkey). On their arrival in Pamphylia, Mark leaves and returns to Jerusalem. Paul and Barnabas then proceed to four cities in Galatia—Antioch in Pisidia, Iconium, Lystra, and Derbe—before retracing their steps in Galatia and returning to Antioch of Syria. Acts 13–14 describes the first journey (see map 1).

After the apostolic conference in Jerusalem in Acts 15, Paul (refusing to take along Mark, who proceeds to Cyprus with Barnabas) takes Silas (or Silvanus) with him and revisits the churches in Galatia (picking up Timothy at Lystra). Guided by the Holy Spirit, Paul proceeds to Europe, preaching at Philippi, Thessalonica, Berea, Athens, and Corinth before returning to Antioch of Syria by way of Ephesus and Jerusalem. Luke relates this trip in Acts 15:36–18:22 (see map 2).

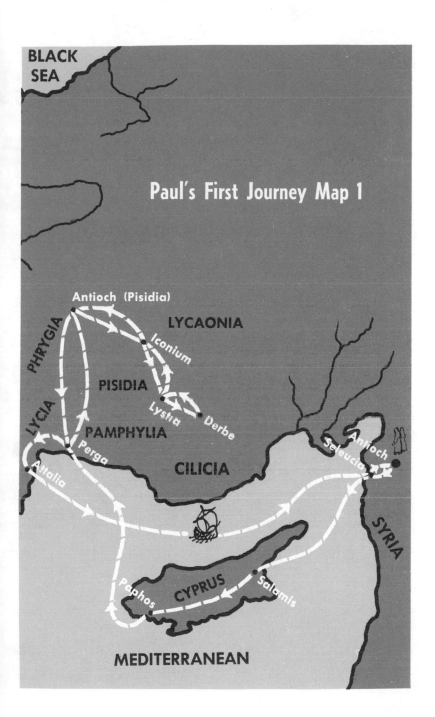

Paul's First Journey Map 1

BLACK SEA

PHRYGIA

LYCIA

PAMPHYLIA

Antioch (Pisidia)

LYCAONIA

Iconium

PISIDIA

Lystra

Derbe

Perga

Attalia

CILICIA

Antioch

Seleucia

SYRIA

Paphos

CYPRUS

Salamis

MEDITERRANEAN

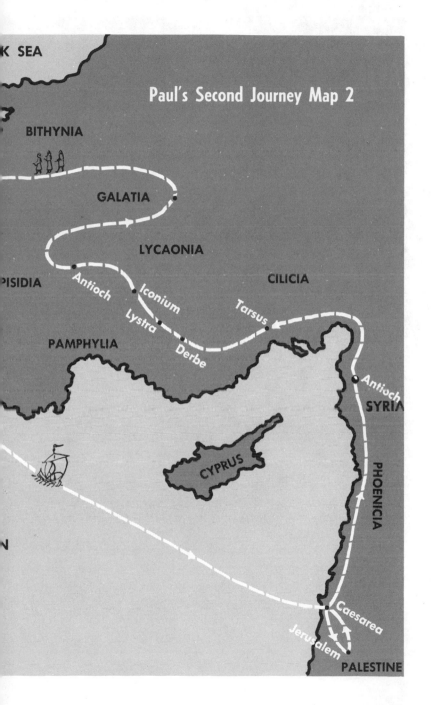

Paul's Second Journey Map 2

K SEA

BITHYNIA

GALATIA

LYCAONIA

PISIDIA

CILICIA

Antioch

Iconium

Lystra

Tarsus

Derbe

PAMPHYLIA

Antioch

SYRIA

CYPRUS

PHOENICIA

Caesarea

Jerusalem

PALESTINE

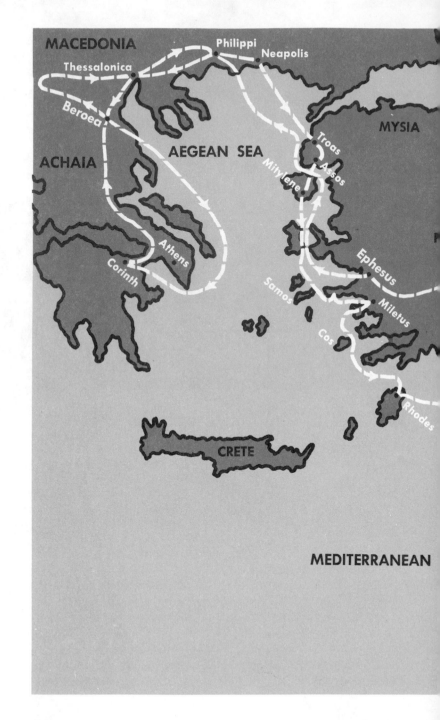

MACEDONIA

Philippi

Neapolis

Thessalonica

Beroea

MYSIA

ACHAIA

AEGEAN SEA

Troas

Assos

Mitylene

Athens

Ephesus

Corinth

Samos

Miletus

Cos

Rhodes

CRETE

MEDITERRANEAN

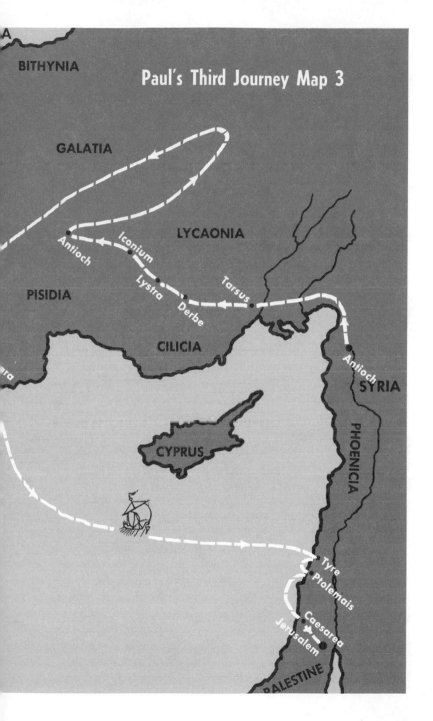

Paul's Third Journey Map 3

BITHYNIA

GALATIA

LYCAONIA

Antioch

Iconium

Lystra

Derbe

Tarsus

PISIDIA

CILICIA

Antioch

SYRIA

CYPRUS

PHOENICIA

Tyre

Ptolemais

Caesarea

Jerusalem

PALESTINE

Rome
ITALY
Puteoli
ADRIATIC
SEA
ILLYRICUM
MACEDONIA
TYRRHENIAN
SEA
ACHAIA
AEG
SICILY
Rhegium
IONIAN SEA
Syracuse
Melita
THE GREAT SEA

Paul's Voyage to Rome **Map 4**

BLACK SEA

PONTUS

BITHYNIA

MYSIA

GALATIA

CAPPADOCIA

LYDIA

PISIDIA

LYCAONIA

CILICIA

PHRYGIA

PAMPHYLIA

SYRIA

LYCIA

Cnidus

Myra

CYPRUS

PHOENICIA

MEDITERRANEAN

Sidon

Tyre

Caesarea

Jerusalem

PALESTINE

EGYPT

On his third journey Paul revisits the churches in Galatia, spends about three years in Ephesus, and then revisits the churches in Europe, finally returning to Jerusalem with a collection from the various churches for the Christians in that city. The third journey is recorded in Acts 18:23–21:17 (see map 3). A brief outline might be helpful:

1st Journey (Acts 13–14): *Galatia*
2d Journey (Acts 15:36–18:22): *Galatia* and *Europe*
3d Journey (Acts 18:23–21:17): *Galatia, Ephesus, Europe.*

The remaining chapters of Acts—in fact, the last quarter of Acts (7 of 28 chapters)—relate Paul's arrest in Jerusalem, his imprisonment in Caesarea for two years, his appearances before Roman officials Felix and Festus and before King Agrippa and Bernice, his trip to Rome after he appealed to Nero's court (see map 4), and his two-year house arrest at Rome. But nothing is specifically stated concerning the outcome of the trial. The reader is left hanging in the air. There are also no conversions (except at Malta) in the last quarter of Acts. These facts should be remembered when one considers the purpose, time, and date of Acts, for the underlying feature of these chapters is that, while the Jewish leaders see Paul as a hostile person, the Roman authorities consistently exonerate him and find nothing in the Christian movement as politically dangerous. The significance to Theophilus, if he also is a Roman official, is very clear and strong, indeed.

Chronology in Acts

In the previous section we did not attach any dates to Paul's activities, for this topic merits separate consideration. The chronology of Acts and of Paul's career can never be exact, for the text does not mention specific dates in relating most of the events. There are, however, three occurrences in Acts that may serve as pegs on which to hang the chronology in general. First and most important is Paul's appearance before Gallio in Corinth toward the end of the second missionary journey (Acts 18:12–17). From an inscription found in Greece around the turn of the century it is clear that Gallio was in office at Corinth in about A.D. 50–51. Two other clues come from the Jewish historian Josephus, who dates the killing of James, son of Zebedee, by Herod (Acts 12:1–2) at A.D. 44 and the famine in Jerusalem (Acts 11:27–30) at A.D. 46.

Before expanding on the general chronology based on these three events, we should mention a problem concerning the interpretation of Galatians 2:1. According to Galatians 1:18 Paul visited Jerusalem three years after his conversion; according to Galatians 2:1 "after fourteen years" he again went to Jerusalem. The question is whether Paul means 14 years after his conversion or 14 years after his first visit to Jerusalem. Furthermore a portion of a year could count as a full year in the calculation in the Roman world. So the time from Paul's conversion to his second visit to Jerusalem could be an interval ranging from 12 to 17 years.

But in spite of the uncertainty in interpreting Galatians 2:1, we may construct the following chronology of Acts and Paul's career:

A.D.		Acts
30	Pentecost	2
	Death of Stephen	7
32	Paul's Conversion	9
44	Death of James	12
46	Famine at Jerusalem	11:27–30; 12:25
47–48	Paul's First Journey	13–14
49	Apostolic Council	15
49–51	Paul's Second Journey	15:36–18:22
51	Paul before Gallio at Corinth	18:12–17
52–56	Paul's Third Journey	18:23–21:17
56	Paul's Arrest at Jerusalem	21:26–23:32
56–58	Paul's Caesarean Imprisonment	23:33–26:32
59	Paul's Voyage to Rome	27:1–28:16
59–61	Paul's First Roman Imprisonment	28:30–31

It must be remembered, however, that these dates are approximations and seem to be correct within a few years either way.

Paul's Visits to Jerusalem

Before leaving the topic of chronology, it may be of interest to list the five visits of Paul to Jerusalem that are mentioned in Acts and to correlate them with the three visits to Jerusalem to which Paul refers in his epistles.

1. Three years after his conversion — Acts 9:26–29 and Gal. 1:18–24
2. Fourteen years after his conversion — Acts 11:27–30 and Gal. 2:1–10
3. For the Apostolic Council — Acts 15:1–29

| 4. At end of his second journey | Acts 18:20–22 |
| 5. At end of his third journey | Acts 21:15–17 and 1 Cor. 16:1–4 |

It should be noted again that this table assumes that Galatians 2:1–10 is to be identified with the famine visit and that it occurred 14 years after Paul's conversion.

The Reliability of Acts

At the beginning of this chapter we noted that Acts is extremely important for three reasons: (1) It is our primary document on the development and expansion of the early church. (2) It assists in understanding the background and order of Paul's letters. (3) It has been the focus of attention by many scholars who challenge the reliability of the New Testament and who point to certain apparent discrepancies between Acts and Paul's epistles. It is this last item that we should now consider.

Some scholars see a discrepancy between Acts and Galatians concerning Paul's visits to Jerusalem (as outlined briefly above). They claim that both Acts 15 and Galatians 2:1–10 refer to the same visit to Jerusalem—for the Apostolic Council—and that these two accounts differ in many details. Acts 15, for example, is a public meeting, while Galatians 2:1–10 refers to a private conference between Paul and some of the apostles. They assert also that Galatians 2 says nothing about the decision concerning abstinence from certain food by Gentiles. These apparent discrepancies, however, disappear when Galatians 2:1–10 is taken as identical to the famine visit recorded in Acts 11:27–30, as we have done in the outline above.

Another charge by some scholars concerns Paul's attitude toward the Old Testament ceremonial law in general and toward circumcision in particular. Paul definitely opposes circumcision in Galatians, but in Acts 16:1–3 Paul has Timothy circumcised, and in Acts 21:23–26 he helps four men keep a ceremonial vow at Jerusalem. The key to this apparent discrepancy is the understanding of the different circumstances involved. Circumcision and the whole ceremonial law are *adiaphora*, that is, they are not forbidden in themselves. Paul states that at times he lived as a Jew and at times as a Gentile (1 Cor. 9:19–23). For certain reasons Paul had Timothy circumcised when Timothy joined him on the second journey, and later Paul helped financially in keeping a vow—to show the Jews that he was not anti-Jewish. But in Galatians, when opponents of the Gospel message of grace demanded circumcision as a condition for Gentiles to become Christians, Paul was forced to take a firm stand to maintain the purity of the Gospel message. The opponents were making an *adiaphoron* a matter of doctrine and were thereby supporting false doctrine. So when the different circumstances are taken into account, the apparent discrepancy between Acts and Galatians disappears.

Finally, scholars who have examined various political and legal details in Acts conclude that the book is extremely reliable. For example, the author makes correct distinctions between the titles of various secular officials. He realizes that Cyprus (13:7) and Achaia (18:12) are senatorial provinces, not imperial provinces, and correctly refers to their rulers as proconsuls rather than legates or procurators. At Philippi the author again uses the correct title for the rulers of a Roman colony (16:20) and his assistants (16:35). At Thessalonica (17:6), Ephesus (19:31, 35), and Malta (28:7) correct titles are also given. Scholars who have checked these details conclude that the author of Acts was a contemporary of Paul and that he carefully investigated such details in order to write an accurate account.

Accuracy in details in Acts is not limited to correct titles for various secular rulers. Other studies indicate that the legal procedures described in Acts fit those of the Roman world in the first century. The consensus of these studies is that, where Acts can be checked, it proves to be a most reliable document. This evidence agrees with the conclusion in our chapter on Luke—that Luke-Acts is a two-volume document composed by a companion of Paul and is correctly assigned by the early church to Luke.

As we now proceed to Paul's Epistles, references to Acts should be helpful.

6. Galatians: Gospel of God's Grace Attacked by Judaism

STUDY QUESTION 1

The usual opening sentence of a letter by Paul.

A. What are the three elements with which Paul customarily begins his letters? See 1 Cor. 1:1–3; 2 Cor. 1:1–2; Eph. 1:1–2; Phil. 1:1–2; Col. 1:1–2; 1 Thess. 1:1; 2 Thess. 1:1–2. Compare also Acts 15:23 and 23:26.

B. Does the fact that Paul begins each epistle with his own name indicate that he was egotistical? Why did Paul and other writers follow this custom?

Paul's Letters

Since Galatians is the first letter by Paul that we are discussing, a word should be said about the form of letters in the Greek and Roman world—particularly about their opening formula. At first it may seem odd that a writer would make his own name the first word in the letter. Today we sign our letters at the end. The reason for the different form among the Greeks and Romans is that they wrote on scrolls. If the name of the writer had been at the end of the letter, the reader would have had to unroll the entire scroll in order to identify the sender. Today we quickly identify the sender by noting a return address on the envelope, a postmark, the letterhead, or the signature at the bottom of the page. Therefore it was as a convenience to the reader that the writer placed his name first, not a mark of egotism.

The first sentence followed a fixed form: (1) the name of the writer and his office or other identification, (2) the name of the addressee or reader, and (3) a wish or greeting of some kind. Acts contains two examples of the fixed form for the beginning of letters: "The apostles, the elders, and the brethren, to the brethren who are of the Gentiles in Antioch, Syria, and Cilicia: Greetings" (15:23). "Claudius Lysias, to the most excellent governor Felix: Greetings" (23:26). Paul follows this form in his epistles with some expansion. After the greeting, he adds a statement of thanksgiving for the readers (in all of his epistles, that is, except Galatians) and usually launches into a doctrinal section followed by a practical section, closing with personal greetings.

The order of the Pauline Epistles in our Bibles is not the order in which Paul wrote them; it was determined according to the length of the letter. First come the letters to various churches, with Romans, the longest, placed at the beginning. Then the other epistles to the churches are arranged in the order of their length: 1 Corinthians, 2 Corinthians, Galatians, Ephesians, Philippians, Colossians, 1 Thessalonians, 2 Thessalonians. After the letters to the churches are the letters to individuals, again arranged according to length— 1 Timothy, 2 Timothy, Titus, and Philemon.

Some students of Scripture see real meaning and value in this traditional order of the letters to churches, for they see in it a logical sequence of instruction, with the doctrine of justification in Romans coming first and the return of Christ in the two epistles to the Thessalonians coming last. Other scholars detect an order based on the experience of salvation: the natural man (Romans), the carnal man (1 and 2 Corinthians, Galatians), the spiritual man (Ephesians, Philippians, Colossians), the end of the church on earth (1 and 2 Thessalonians).

But regardless of the meaning or value of the traditional or canonical order, we shall study Paul's epistles in the order in which they were written, as far as we can determine. In some cases the time of their composition is clear from the text (for example, Romans and the two epistles to the Corinthians). In other cases specialists do not agree on the dates of composition. One of these letters is Galatians, which many consider the earliest, although not all scholars agree.

The opening of Galatians.

A. **How does the opening sentence of Galatians (1:1–6) compare with the above introductory formula? What similarity do you find? What differences do you see in Gal. 1:1–6?**

B. **What two important matters seem to be on Paul's mind in Gal. 1:1–5?**

Galatians 1:1–6

The introductory verses of Galatians show that it is a unique epistle in several respects. Normally Paul begins his letters in this way: "Paul, an apostle . . . to the church at . . . grace to you and peace . . . . I thank . . . ." In Gal. 1:1–6, however, we note several differences. It is addressed to the churches of Galatia, which means that it is a circular letter, intended for a group of churches. But more important, there is an abrupt assertion of authority inserted after the opening words, "Paul, an apostle." He immediately makes it clear to the readers that his commission as an apostle comes directly from Jesus Christ and God the Father—not from any human person or persons. Apparently Paul's authority was being challenged and questioned. Likewise, after "Grace to you and peace . . ." Paul inserts a brief summary of the Gospel in verse 4: "who gave Himself for our sins, that He might deliver us from this present evil age." Apparently the truth and purity of the Gospel message was also being challenged. These two points—Paul's authority and the purity of the Gospel—were so serious that Paul does not include his usual statement of thanksgiving in this letter to the Galatian congregations. Instead of "I thank," he asserts: "I marvel . . ." (v. 6). In brief, Paul writes to the Galatians with a heavy heart because two important matters are at stake, his authority as an apostle and the purity of the Gospel. The entire epistle, as we shall see, elaborates on these two items.

STUDY QUESTION 3

Read Acts 13 and 14, which relate Paul's first journey. There are good indications that Paul wrote Galatians

to the churches in the southern part of the Roman prov-
ince of Galatia—Pisidian Antioch, Iconium, Lystra, and
Derbe.

A. Compare Gal. 4:14 with Acts 14:8–18.
B. Compare Gal. 6:17 with Acts 14:19–20.
C. Compare Gal. 4:13 with Acts 13:13–14; 15:36–41.

Galatia

Paul addresses this letter "to the churches of Galatia" (Gal. 1:2). The exact destination is still disputed among scholars, since the term Galatia could have one of two meanings. It could refer to a settlement in north central Turkey, where a group of Gauls from modern France settled a few centuries before the birth of Christ. It could also refer to southern Turkey, which was a part of the Roman province of Galatia at the time of Paul. Without engaging in a lengthy debate on the pros and cons of each interpretation, we prefer the view that Paul is addressing the group of churches that he founded on his first journey described in Acts 13–14. That is, we interpret the term "churches in Galatia" as referring specifically to the four cities in southern Turkey: Pisidian Antioch, Iconium, Lystra, and Derbe.

We might mention briefly several passages in Galatians that appear to substantiate this choice. Paul writes: "You know that because of physical infirmity I preached the Gospel to you at the first" (4:13). According to Acts (13:13–14) Mark left the expedition when Paul and Barnabas went from the lowlands of Pamphylia to Pisidian Antioch, which was a more healthful region. It seems that the decision to go to this higher region involved a change from the original plan and gave Mark a reason for returning to Jerusalem. In that case, the question of the reason for the change in itinerary arises. It is quite reasonable that Paul, who probably planned initially to proceed west to Ephesus, was forced by some illness such as malaria to go north to a more healthful area. So he reminds the readers of Galatians that he came to them originally as a result of a physical infirmity or bodily ailment.

In the following verse (Gal. 4:14) Paul states that the readers received him "as an angel of God." The Greek word for "angel" could also be translated "messenger." This translation could refer to an incident at Lystra on Paul's first journey (Acts 14:8–18). There was an old legend in Greek mythology, known no doubt to everyone in Lystra, that told of a visit by Zeus and his messenger Hermes to that city. Since Zeus and Hermes came in human form, they were refused hospitality by all except one poor couple, who were rewarded for their generosity. According to Acts, the people of Lystra thought that Zeus and Hermes had returned in the form of Barnabas and Paul, respectively, since they healed a cripple in their midst. The citizens of Lystra summoned the local priest of Zeus, who prepared sacrifices to honor the two supposedly divine visitors. Paul and Barnabas finally restrained the crowd from offering sacrifices to them. In Galatians Paul is reminding the people of Lystra that they at first had regarded Paul as Zeus's messenger, Hermes.

In the concluding verses of Galatians Paul says: "I bear in my body the marks of the Lord Jesus" (6:17). He seems to be reminding his readers at Lystra of what happened to him before he left their town on his first journey (Acts 14:19–20). The refusal to accept their sacrifices may have offended the people of Lystra. At least we are told in Acts that Jewish leaders from Pisidian Antioch and Iconium arrived at Lystra and turned public opinion against Paul, causing him to be stoned and to be dragged outside the city and left for dead. In Galatians, Paul seems to be telling the readers that he still had bruises and scars from his stoning at Lystra.

STUDY QUESTION 4

The great influx of non-Jews into the early church gave rise to the problems addressed in Galatians. Trace the influx in the following passages: Acts 8:4–25; 10:1– 11:18; 11:19–26; 15:1.

Occasion

To understand the occasion for Paul's Epistle to the Galatians, we should review briefly the events in the early church that led to the Apostolic Council in Jerusalem reported in Acts 15. In the first seven chapters of Acts the preaching of the Gospel is confined to Jerusalem. Then after a persecution in Jerusalem, Philip preaches in Samaria (Acts 8:4–25), and Peter proclaims the message to Cornelius and his household in Caesarea (Acts 10–11). At this point apparently only a small number of Gentiles had accepted the faith, coming either directly from paganism or as proselytes of Judaism.

Some years later, when missionaries travelled to Antioch in Syria (Acts 11:19–26), a great number of Greeks "turned to the Lord." In fact, the church at Jerusalem sent Barnabas to Antioch, and he fetched Paul from Tarsus, so that for a whole year they did missionary work at Antioch largely among the Greeks.

The large influx of Greek believers at Antioch, where they were first called Christians, no doubt alarmed the Jewish believers at Jerusalem. They feared that soon the Gentiles might outnumber the Jews in the early church. After working for a full year at Antioch, Barnabas and Paul depart on the first missionary journey, no doubt sponsored by the Christians at Antioch. They visit the island of Cyprus and then the four cities in Galatia. By the conclusion of the first journey the number of Greek converts had increased considerably, as the account in Acts 13–14 indicates. Some Jewish Christians in Jerusalem became so concerned that they went to Antioch in Syria after Paul and Barnabas had returned and claimed: "Unless you are circumcised according to the custom of Moses, you cannot be saved" (Acts 15:1).

STUDY QUESTION 5

Paul's opponents were attacking him on two counts: (1) his authority and (2) his message.

A. *How did Paul answer the first charge in Gal. 1:6–2:21?*

B. *How did Paul answer the second charge in Gal. 3:1–4:31?*

These Jewish Christians, or others of similar conviction, promote their views in the churches of Galatia, which Paul and Barnabas had recently founded. Their claim is at least twofold. One point they try to make is that Paul did not give the complete message to the Gentiles. What he said about salvation through faith in Jesus, they assert, is true, but that is not the whole story. In addition to faith, circumcision and the keeping of the ceremonial law are required. The other point they try to make is that Paul did not preach the whole truth because he received his message secondhand from the apostles who had known Jesus in the flesh and that therefore he had not comprehended the message completely.

We can imagine Paul's reaction when the news reaches him, possibly at Antioch, of the claims that some Jewish Christians are making in these recently founded congregations in Galatia. He is in a very emotional frame of mind. He takes time immediately to write to the churches in Galatia to answer the two main charges leveled against him.

Point One: He received his commission as an apostle directly from God on the road to Damascus and was not dependent on any apostle at Jerusalem for his information. In fact, he had been at Jerusalem only twice since his conversion—the first time for only two weeks, three years after his conversion, and the second time some years later when he consulted privately with James, Peter, and John, only to discover that his preaching agreed with theirs. How could these people from Judea claim that Paul received his message secondhand? In fact, on one occasion he had to correct an erring Peter.

Point Two: The purity of the Gospel message is at stake. Anyone who *demands* circumcision for membership in the Christian church is destroying the Gospel. Such a person, even if it be an angel from heaven, is accursed. The Galatians should look at their own experience. They should also consider Abraham, who was counted righteous through faith. The law, which came 400 years later, cannot annul God's promises to Abraham and his descendants.

Paul is so anxious to make these two points that he composes his usual introductory verses with abrupt assertions that bear on his arguments (1:1, 4) and omits the customary thanksgiving.

Extended Outline

To follow Paul's argumentation against the charges of his opponents, we shall present an extended outline of Galatians.

  I. Introduction (1:1–5). Already in the salutation Paul inserts references to the charges of the opponents:
     A. His apostleship comes from God, not from the apostles.
     B. The risen Jesus Christ is the total essence of the Gospel.
  II. Personal Argument (1:6–2:21). The expanded argument to the charge that he received his message secondhand:

A. Paul received his call and authority directly from God, not from the apostles at Jerusalem, where he visited for only two weeks, three years after he began preaching (1:6–24).

B. When he visited Jerusalem again, 14 years after his conversion, the leaders of the church at Jerusalem recognized that the message preached by Paul was the same message they were proclaiming (2:1–10).

C. On one occasion at Antioch in Syria, instead of receiving instruction from Peter, Paul was forced to correct Peter's actions publicly (2:11–14).

D. Paul summarizes the Gospel message (2:15–21).

III. Doctrinal Argument (3:1–4:31). The expanded argument in answer to the charge that faith alone is insufficient and must be augmented by circumcision and the keeping of the Old Testament ceremonial law:

A. Three witnesses to the function of Law and Gospel are:
   1. the experience of the Galatians themselves (3:1–5);
   2. the witness of the Old Testament concerning Abraham (3:6–9); and
   3. the witness of the Old Testament law itself, which brings curses (3:10–14).

B. The relationship between Law and promise shows:
   1. that the Law did not cancel the promise (3:15–18);
   2. that the purpose of the Law is to convict us of sin (3:19–22); and
   3. that the promise leads us to Christ (3:23–29).

C. Three examples that salvation comes from God's grace are:
   1. Israel under the Law is like a minor heir, a child without liberty; freedom comes through Christ (4:1–11);
   2. the Galatians in their initial reaction to the Gospel (4:12–20);
   3. the sons of Abraham, one born to slavery and the other to freedom as a result of promise (4:21–31).

IV. Practical Applications (5:1–6:10). Christian freedom under the Gospel.

A. The meaning of freedom under the Gospel; it is liberty, not license (5:1–24).

B. Concrete examples of Christian freedom (5:25–6:10).

V. Conclusion (6:11–18). Paul's summary emphasizes the importance of the subject and the selfish motives of his opponents.

STUDY QUESTION 6

Paul in Galatians does not cite the decision of the Apostolic Council in Acts 15. What may this fact indicate about Paul himself?

Paul's Conviction

Paul's Epistle to the Galatians, although written in a state of stress brought on by the charges of his opponents, manifests a clear and logical train of thought. He is writing on a topic that he was forced to think through carefully under the guidance of the Holy Spirit immediately after his conversion. During his so-called "silent years" (at least eight years not described by Acts) in Tarsus Paul became convinced of the basic truth of the Gospel of faith, not of works. It is that Gospel that he shared with the leaders at Jerusalem and proclaimed on his first journey.

When his opponents began infiltrating the newly founded churches in Galatia, Paul could have waited quietly for the meeting of the Apostolic Council and then calmly relayed that decision to the churches in Galatia. But he did not wait—assuming the sequence of events that we prefer. He could not delay when he was dealing with a conflict that concerned the essence of the Gospel. At once, before the Apostolic Council assembled, Paul wrote the letter to the Galatians, wishing to nip in the bud the false charges of his opponents. False teaching must be attacked immediately. He did not wait to take shelter in a decree of a church council but dealt with the matter at once with courage and assurance.

7. *1 and 2 Thessalonians: Gospel of God's Grace and Persecution*

STUDY QUESTION 1

How do the following passages help to fix the time and place of 1 and 2 Thessalonians: 1 Thess. 1:1; 2 Thess. 1:1; Acts 15:40–41; 16:1–4; 18:1–5; 1 Thess. 3:1–7?

Time and Place

The opening sentences of 1 Thessalonians and of 2 Thessalonians assist in setting the time and place of composition for these two epistles. In each letter Silvanus (the Roman name for Silas) and Timothy are with Paul. Since Acts relates that Paul began his second journey with Silas (15:40–41) and was joined by Timothy at Lystra (16:1–4), these two documents were composed during Paul's second missionary journey—sometime after Paul established a Christian congregation at Thessalonica.

During the second journey Paul revisits the churches in Galatia and preaches the Gospel in Europe—at Philippi, Thessalonica, Berea, Athens, and Corinth. At Athens Paul instructs Timothy to visit the Christians at Thessalonica and to report back to him, which Timothy does at Corinth (Acts 18:1–5; 1 Thess. 3:1–7). We conclude, therefore, that Paul writes these two letters to the Thessalonians from Corinth. Since his stay at Corinth coincides with the proconsulship of Gallio, whose rule in Achaia is dated around A.D. 50–51, the time of the writing of these two epistles is fairly definite. Accordingly, these two documents were composed at Corinth about A.D. 50–51—that is, about 20 years after Jesus' resurrection.

Thessalonica

At the time of Paul Thessalonica was a prosperous seaport. It was also strategic for overland commerce, since a famous road (*Via*

Egnatia) went through the city, connecting the Adriatic to Byzantium (modern Istanbul). Even today it is a flourishing city (Salonika) second only to Athens in Greece.

In Roman times Thessalonica was the capital of the Roman province of Macedonia (northern Greece) and became the residence of the Roman governor. Augustus rewarded its loyalty to him by making it a "free city." That is, it was self-governing in all its internal affairs. There was no garrison of Roman soldiers. Citizens had the right of holding assembly and appointing magistrates. Those on the highest board of magistrates were called "politarchs." Luke's use of this title in the Greek text (Acts 17:6) has been questioned, but the discovery of inscriptions has proved Luke's historical accuracy.

Most of the inhabitants of Thessalonica were Greeks. There was a large Jewish colony there also, no doubt attracted by the commercial advantages of the town. A large number of Gentiles frequented the Jewish synagogue.

STUDY QUESTION 2

Paul's relation with the Thessalonians. Read Acts 17:1–15.

A. What was the reaction of Paul's opponents and their charge against him? See Acts 17:5–10; 17:13; 17:7.

B. How does 1 Thess. 1:9 agree with Acts 17:4 concerning one type of believer in Thessalonica?

C. Who supported Paul financially? See 1 Thess. 2:9.

The Origin of the Church

The origin of the church at Thessalonica is related in Acts 17:1–10. When Paul, Silas (Silvanus), and Timothy left Philippi, where they had been beaten and imprisoned, they passed through two towns (Amphipolis and Apollonia) and settled in Thessalonica, no doubt because this city had a synagogue. On three successive Sabbath days Paul argued with those who attended the synagogue, trying to show that Jesus was the promised Messiah. The result was that Paul convinced some Jews, a large number of Greeks, and some wives of the leaders in the city of the truth of his message.

When he was forced to abandon contact with the synagogue, Paul apparently worked out of a house owned by a certain Jason. It is clear that Paul remained in Thessalonica longer than three weeks, for in writing to the Philippians (4:16) he says that the church at Philippi sent him financial assistance twice while he was in Thessalonica. The length of Paul's stay in Thessalonica may have been several months. During this period more converts from the Greeks were added to the church, for Paul refers to those who "turned to God from idols" (1:9).

Paul finally was forced to leave Thessalonica because of the opposition from the unbelieving Jews. These Jews assaulted the house of Jason and dragged Jason and others before the rulers of the city. The charge was that the Christians "are all acting contrary to the decrees of Caesar, saying that there is another king—Jesus" (Acts 17:7). The riot and the charge were serious threats to the free status of the city. The rulers had Jason post a bond that the incident would not happen again. But the settlement made it impossible for Paul and his companions to continue their work at Thessalonica, for the Jews would be certain to raise another uproar if Paul continued to work there. The Christians asked Paul and his companions to leave. They left reluctantly under the cover of darkness (Acts 17:10) after they had appointed elders to lead the new congregation (1 Thess. 5:12–13).

The Occasion for 1 Thessalonians

One of the main reasons for Paul's writing 1 Thessalonians may be summarized in a single word—persecution. Paul came to Thessalonica after suffering persecution (beating and imprisonment) at Philippi. He was forced to leave Thessalonica as a result of persecution. And what is more, persecution continued from the Jews at Thessalonica. Jews from that synagogue followed Paul to Berea and stirred up antagonism there (Acts 17:10–13). Because Paul knew that persecution continued to be a problem at Thessalonica, he sent Timothy back there to find out what the situation was (1 Thess. 3:1–5). After Timothy visited Thessalonica, he caught up with Paul at Corinth and reported what he had discovered (Acts 18:1, 5).

Besides being concerned about Jewish persecution at Thessalonica, Paul realized that the Thessalonian Christians might misunderstand his sudden departure. In the Greek and Roman world there were numerous traveling charlatans who would remain in a town for a short time in order to make financial profit from their instruction in philosophy, public speaking, and the art of persuasion. After a brief stay they would move on to another town and not be heard from again. Paul realized that some Thessalonians might include Paul in this category, for he did leave suddenly after a brief stay. To counteract such thoughts Paul takes pains to show that he had not been interested in personal financial gain, for he recalls that he had supported himself by manual labor during his stay at Thessalonica (1 Thess. 2:9).

STUDY QUESTION 3

The topics in 1 Thessalonians.

A. **How does Paul show good psychology in 1 Thess. 1:2–10?**

B. **Why does Paul defend his motives in 1 Thess. 2:1–16?**

C. **Why was Paul concerned about the Thessalonian Christians? See 1 Thess. 2:17–3:13.**

D. **What moral advice does Paul give in 1 Thess. 4:1–12?**

E. **What questions are raised about Jesus' second coming in 1 Thess. 4:13–5:11?**

Content of 1 Thessalonians

Paul's tone is warm and confident, thankful for the good report from Timothy that the preaching there was not in vain and that it had spread throughout Macedonia (northern Greece) and Achaia (southern Greece). What happened at Thessalonica was the work of God. What else could explain the firmness of this little group, persecuted and deprived of its teachers (1:2–10)?

In recalling his work at Thessalonica Paul responds to the attacks of the leaders of the synagogue. These enemies were attempting to vilify Paul's character and motives. So he devotes the rest of the first half of the epistle to a defense against these detractors (2:1–3:13). He reminds the Thessalonians that he was not an itinerant teacher, peddling a deceptive message, but that he had been willing to face more trouble, having just come from persecution at Philippi. He never used flattery or tried to get money from them.

He refused financial support, working night and day in order not to be a burden to anyone. He also is grateful to God because the Thessalonians exhibited faithfulness to the Gospel and patience in the face of persecution—as did the Christians in Judea. Paul regrets that he could not come in person, since Satan hindered this wish. Therefore he had sent Timothy, who brought back a basically favorable report.

In 1 Thessalonians, as elsewhere, Paul practices sound psychology. He first accents the positive, mentioning the good points among the Thessalonian Christians in the first three chapters. By this positive approach, he no doubt wins over his readers' good will so that they are prepared for some admonitions and suggestions for improvement. These admonitions come in the last two chapters of 1 Thessalonians.

Paul's first admonition concerns sexual matters. In Greek and Roman society sexual behavior was almost a matter of indifference. Pagan sexual habits fell far short of Jewish and Christian standards. Paul is compelled, therefore, to remind some of the Greek Christians at Thessalonica not to return to their old ways of immorality (4:1–8). He also encourages them to continue their brotherly and orderly life (4:9–12).

Paul's teaching concerning the Lord's return apparently had not been fully understood. Or perhaps he was forced to leave Thessalonica before he had an opportunity to give complete instruction on this topic. At any rate, two problems arose in regard to this subject (4:13–5:11).

One problem concerned those Christians who had died recently—probably between Paul's departure and the composition of the epistle. Will Christians who die before Christ comes again be at a disadvantage? By no means, answers Paul. First the dead will be raised when Jesus comes; then they, together with those Christians who are still alive, will join the Lord and enjoy His presence.

The other problem concerned the time of Jesus' coming. Paul assures the readers that no one knows the time, for Christ will return suddenly and unexpectedly. We do not need to know the time, but we must be ready at all times.

Paul then adds various exhortations on congregational life (5:12–22).

Outline of 1 Thessalonians

A. Thanksgiving and congratulations (1:2–10)
B. Paul's message and motive (2:1–16)
C. Subsequent events (2:17–3:13)
III. Admonitions (4:1–5:22)
A. Exhortation on morality (4:1–12)
B. Two questions on Christ's coming (4:13–5:11)
C. Exhortations on congregational life (5:12–22)
IV. Conclusion (5:23–28)

STUDY QUESTION 4

Passages in 1 Thessalonians that apparently caused concerns among the Thessalonians: 1 Thess. 1:10; 2:19; 3:13; 4:15; 5:2; 5:23. Note the frequency of references to the same event (six times in five brief chapters).

The Occasion for 2 Thessalonians

Paul wrote 2 Thessalonians, the shortest of his letters to congregations, also from Corinth on his second journey a short time after he wrote 1 Thessalonians. What caused him to write a second time so soon (within a few weeks to a couple of months) was apparently a misunderstanding by some Christians at Thessalonica concerning the second coming of Christ, mentioned a number of times in his first document.

In 1 Thessalonians Paul refers frequently to Jesus' second coming, called in Greek *parousia*. If we were to receive such a letter today, what would the effect be? Would we also suppose that the writer was trying to tell us something through the frequent references to Jesus' *parousia?* Let us review for a moment Paul's statements in 1 Thessalonians:

. . . to wait for His Son from heaven, whom He raised from the dead, even Jesus who delivers us from the wrath to come. (1:10)

For what is our hope, or joy, or crown of rejoicing? Is it not even you in the presence of our Lord Jesus Christ at His coming? (2:19)

. . . so that He may establish your hearts blameless in holiness before our God and Father at the coming of our Lord Jesus Christ with all His saints. (3:13)

We who are alive and remain until the coming of the Lord will by no means precede those who are asleep. (4:15)

You yourselves know perfectly that the day of the Lord so comes as a thief in the night. (5:2)

May your whole spirit, soul, and body be preserved blameless at the coming of our Lord Jesus Christ. (5:23)

What would our reaction be to a letter that refers at least six times to Jesus' second coming? The Christians at Thessalonica apparently were astonished at the frequent references to Christ's *parousia* in 1 Thessalonians. The effect was not the same on all of them. Whoever delivered 1 Thessalonians, whose identity we are not told, reported to Paul on the effect of the letter while Paul was still at Corinth. Therefore Paul deals in his second letter with the misunderstandings of the Thessalonians concerning Christ's second coming.

STUDY QUESTION 5

Paul's treatment of the concerns about Jesus' parousia.

A. How does Paul respond to those who feared that they would not be "blameless" at Jesus' second coming? See 1 Thess. 3:13; 5:23; 2 Thess. 2:13–17.

B. How does Paul respond to those who thought that Jesus would return any day? See 2 Thess. 2:1–12; 3:6–15.

Content of 2 Thessalonians

Some Thessalonians had become fearful and alarmed after reading the first letter. No doubt they misunderstood two sentences by Paul. Some understood the one statement (3:13) to mean that they were expected to be "blameless in holiness" when Jesus comes again. The other statement (5:23) likewise demanded that Christians must be "blameless at the coming of our Lord Jesus Christ." These two statements frightened some Thessalonians. How could anyone stand "blameless in holiness" or be kept "blameless" before Jesus on the day of the final judgment?

Paul calms the fears of these Christians in 2 Thess. 2:13–17. He emphasizes that they are "beloved" by the Lord because "God from the beginning chose" them. That is, their salvation does not depend on their sinlessness but on God's election. Furthermore, Paul assures these people that they are saved through sanctification by the Holy Spirit and faith in the truth of the Gospel. The Gospel has called them so that they may obtain the glory of our Lord Jesus Christ. Our Lord Jesus Christ and God our Father loves them and gives them eternal comfort and good hope through God's grace—in no way dependent on their being sinless and perfect. Paul no doubt has these people in mind also when he extends comfort and assurance in 1:3–12.

The first letter had a different effect on other members of the congregation. They concluded that if Jesus was coming in the immediate future, as they inferred from Paul's frequent references to it, it would be advisable for them to give up their gainful employment and get ready for Christ's *parousia*. As a result they became idle and disorderly, depending on the charity of the church. To this group at Thessalonica Paul writes that the "man of sin" or the "lawless one" must come before Jesus' *parousia* would take place (2:1–12). Paul later gives guidance to correct their disorderly life (3:6–15).

Outline of 2 Thessalonians

    I. Opening greeting (1:1–2)
    II. Thanksgiving and encouragement (1:3–12)
        A. Steadfastness under persecution (1:3–4)
        B. Encouragement concerning the final judgment (1:5–12)
    III. Admonitions concerning the *parousia* (2:1–17)
        A. Man of sin or of lawlessness must come first (2:1–12)
        B. *Parousia* means salvation for the elect (2:13–17)
    IV. Exhortations (3:1–15)
        A. To pray (3:1–5)
        B. To correct the idle and disorderly (3:6–15)
    V. Conclusion (3:16–18)

STUDY QUESTION 6

*Do 1 and 2 Thessalonians disagree on the time of Jesus'
second coming?*

A. *What is your opinion after reading 1 Thess. 4:13–
5:11 and 2 Thess. 2:1–12?*

B. *Do the words of Jesus help solve the problem? See
Matt. 24:36 and 24:6–8.*

2 Thessalonians 2:1–12

We should say something about one of the more difficult passages in Paul's 13 epistles—probably one that even Peter found hard to understand (2 Peter 3:16). In 2 Thess. 2:1–12 Paul states that before Christ's second coming there will be a great and final rebellion against God, headed by an individual opposed to God. Various suggestions have been made concerning the identity of the "man of sin" or the "lawless one"—Nero, the papacy (as was thought especially at the time of the Reformation), Napoleon, Hitler, Stalin.

But what seems more important is the relation of this passage to the tone of the first letter. Some scholars see a discrepancy between 1 Thess. 4:13–5:11, which teaches the imminence of Jesus' return as a thief in the night, and 2 Thess. 2:1–12, which states that certain events must occur before Jesus returns. The difficulty is more apparent than real. Both statements are true: We do not know the exact time, so Jesus will come as a thief in the night, and certain events must also precede Christ's *parousia* as signs. The double emphasis is similar to the double emphasis found in Jesus' own teaching about His return. In Matt. 24:36 He states: "Of that day and hour no one knows, no, not even the angels of heaven, but My Father only." Thus it comes as a thief in the night. But in the same chapter Jesus also refers to events such as wars, famines, and earthquakes that must precede the *parousia* (Matt. 24:6–8).

8. 1 Corinthians: Gospel of God's Grace and Human Wisdom

STUDY QUESTION 1

How do the following passages help to fix the time and place of 1 Corinthians: 1 Cor. 16:8; 16:5; 16:19; Acts 18:24–26?

Time and Place

We have noted that Paul wrote Galatians soon after the conclusion of his first journey and that he wrote 1 and 2 Thessalonians toward the end of his second journey. Several years passed before the writing of 1 Corinthians. It is clear from the last chapter that Paul wrote this epistle from Ephesus on his third journey. He is at Ephesus, where he intends to remain until Pentecost (16:8); he plans to visit Corinth after he passes through Macedonia (16:5); and he sends greetings from the churches of Asia (16:19), of which province Ephesus was the leading city, together with greetings from Aquila and Priscilla (Prisca), who were living at Ephesus (Acts 18:24–26). This information in 1 Corinthians fits perfectly into Luke's account of Paul's movements during his third journey (Acts 18:22–21:17).

We have placed the Thessalonian correspondence around A.D. 50–51, near the close of the second journey. On the third journey Paul revisited the churches in Galatia and then spent about three years in Ephesus before revisiting churches in Europe that he had founded on the second journey. Since 1 Corinthians was composed at Ephesus, the date of writing would be sometime around A.D. 53–54—that is, three or four years after the correspondence with Thessalonica.

STUDY QUESTION 2

The church at Corinth.

A. **Who founded this church? See Acts 18:1–19; 1 Cor. 3:6, 10; 4:15.**

B. **Why did Paul stay at Corinth so long? See Acts 18:9–10; 18:1–3; 2 Cor. 11:9 and Acts 18:5 and Phil. 4:15; 1 Cor. 9:24–27.**

C. **What conclusion may be drawn about Sosthenes from Acts 18:17 and 1 Cor. 1:1, if we assume that the same person is meant in both passages?**

Corinth

To understand the Corinthian correspondence we should be acquainted with some information on the city itself and the church at Corinth. Already during the days of Homer, Corinth was an important city. Homer referred to it as "wealthy Corinth." It lay in ruins for a hundred years after being destroyed by the Romans in 146 B.C. In 46 B.C. Julius Caesar rebuilt the city as a Roman colony. Augustus made it the capital of the province of Achaia (southern Greece) and the residence of the proconsul. Thus the rebuilt city of Corinth was less than a hundred years old when Paul first travelled there.

Situated on a narrow isthmus, it was important to commerce between the peninsula and the mainland of Greece (north and south) and also to commerce between Asia and Italy (east and west). As a commercial city Corinth was very cosmopolitan. Politically Corinth was controlled by a Roman minority. Most of the people were Greeks. Its opportunities for financial benefit attracted a large colony of Jews. Also in this harbor town would be found Syrians, Asiatics, and Egyptians. Athletes would come to Corinth to participate in the Isthmian Games, which were held every two years.

Numerous temples to Greek gods and goddesses—Athena, Apollo, Poseidon, Hermes—dotted the city; there was also a Pantheon or temple of "all the gods" as well as a temple of Aesculapius, a god of healing. The most famous temple in Corinth was dedicated to Aphrodite (or Venus), the goddess of love, and traditionally had a thousand prostitutes. In fact, morals were so low in Corinth that the terms "to Corinthianize" and "a Corinthian" meant "to engage in prostitution" and "a prostitute," respectively.

The population of Corinth at the time of Paul's visits is estimated at six to seven hundred thousand people, about two-thirds of them slaves. Its commercial wealth also brought culture. Corinthian pottery and Corinthian bronze art objects were famous throughout the Mediterranean world. Corinth also produced some noted painters and a distinct type of temple architecture. Although not distinguished in the area of literature and philosophy in comparison to Athens, the Corinthians did show an interest in knowledge or wisdom, as did Greek culture in general.

What an unlikely place for the Gospel message to take root! Yet Paul on his first visit remained at Corinth at least a year and a half (Acts 18:11). Why did Paul work so long at this center of human wisdom? Several factors should be considered. First and foremost is the fact that the Lord so directed him. After Paul experienced opposition from the Jewish synagogue, we read: "Now the Lord spoke to Paul in the night by a vision, 'Do not be afraid, but speak, and do not keep silent; for I am with you, and no one will attack you to hurt you; for I have many people in this city' " (Acts 18:9–10). Second, the hospitality of Aquila and Priscilla, who were of the same vocation, brought about a harmonious arrangement for a longer stay at Corinth (Acts 18:1–3). Third, a financial gift from Macedonia (no doubt from Philippi) reached Paul through Silas and Timothy while he was at Corinth, making a longer stay feasible (2 Cor. 11:9; Acts 18:5; Phil. 4:15). A fourth factor could concern the Isthmian Games. That Paul knew quite a bit about such athletic games is clear from 1 Cor. 9:24–27. Arriving at Corinth in A.D. 50 and realizing that the Isthmian Games would be held at Corinth in the spring of A.D. 51, Paul could have seen a wonderful opportunity to preach Christ crucified to the numerous competitors and spectators assembled from all of Greece—people who could carry the Gospel to many towns throughout the Mediterranean that Paul himself had never visited.

The Origin of the Church

According to Acts 18:1–19 and 1 Cor. 3:6, 10 and 4:15 Paul was the founder of the church at Corinth. On his arrival he met Aquila (also a tentmaker) and his wife Priscilla, who as Jews had been banished recently from Rome and who showed Paul hospitality. Every Sabbath Paul (no doubt accompanied by Aquila and Priscilla) proclaimed the Gospel message in the local synagogue to the Jews and the Greek proselytes who attended. Soon fierce opposition from the Jews caused Paul to withdraw from the synagogue and to establish headquarters in a house next door. While most of the converts seem to have been Greek, we are told specifically that Crispus, formerly a ruler of the synagogue, accepted the Christian faith (Acts 18:8) and that he was baptized by Paul (1 Cor. 1:14).

The success of Paul's ministry in Corinth continued to arouse the anger of the Jews. After Paul had worked in Corinth for some months, a new Roman proconsul named Gallio arrived. The Jews brought charges against Paul before Gallio, accusing Paul of teaching a type of worship that was contrary to their law. Since the charge involved a religious argument rather than a civil matter, Gallio refused to judge the case and dismissed the court. In fact, the Roman soldiers beat a Jewish ruler of the synagogue, Sosthenes, when he refused to leave the court—an incident that Gallio did not try to stop (Acts 18:17).

It is interesting to note that as Acts 18:8 mentions Paul's conversion of a ruler of the synagogue named Crispus and 1 Cor. 1:14 refers to Paul's baptizing of Crispus, so Sosthenes is mentioned in both Acts and 1 Corinthians. In Acts 18.17 Sosthenes is a ruler of the synagogue opposed to Paul; in 1 Cor. 1:1 Paul includes Sosthenes as his fellow Christian. The implication seems to be that Sosthenes, an opponent during Paul's ministry, was converted during the ministry of Paul's successor, Apollos. Now Sosthenes and Paul are together at Ephesus, where Paul is composing 1 Corinthians. The Corinthians, who are taking sides on the basis of personalities some preferring Paul and others preferring Apollos (1 Cor. 1:10–17)—should stop and think. Sosthenes and Paul are together, preaching the same Gospel. Sosthenes learned the Gospel from Apollos, Paul's successor at Corinth, which indicates that Apollos and Paul are preachers of the same message. That is the important matter, not the different personality traits of the preacher.

The members of the Corinthian congregation had a varied background. They were primarily Greeks, Romans, and Jews. While some Jews had been converted (Acts 18:8), the majority of the members were Gentiles (1 Cor. 12:2). A number of the Corinthian Christians had Roman names: Crispus and Gaius (1 Cor. 1:14), Fortunatus (1 Cor. 16:17), Justus (Acts 18:7), Tertius and Quartus (Rom. 16:22–23; Romans was written from Corinth). The membership at Corinth also varied socially. A few were of noble rank, but the majority were from the lower strata of society (1 Cor. 1:26–31)—no doubt workers in the dockyards, pottery works, bronze foundries, bakeries, and other shops. The church included slaves and former slaves as well as free citizens (1 Cor. 7:21–22;

12:13). Although some may have been wealthy, most seemed to have been poor (11:21–22). Some members apparently had previously led openly sinful lives (1 Cor. 6:9–11), and some of the old habits crept into the church and caused concern (5:1, 9–13).

The overriding characteristic of the Corinthian church, however, seems to have been the admiration of human wisdom, a trait characteristic of Greek culture throughout its history. Paul reminds the people that his approach was different—not based on "persuasive words of human wisdom" (1 Cor. 2:4)—because his goal was that their "faith should not be in the wisdom of men but in the power of God" (2:5). The Corinthian love for human wisdom may have been one reason that Paul's successor at Corinth was Apollos, "an eloquent man," a native of Alexandria (Acts 18:24). "He vigorously refuted the Jews publicly, showing from the Scriptures that Jesus is the Christ" (18:28).

STUDY QUESTION 3

The occasion for writing this letter.

A. How did Paul hear about the situation at Corinth? See 1 Cor. 1:11; 7:1 (cf. 8:1; 12:1; 16:1); 16:17.

B. What serious problems had arisen at Corinth? See 1 Cor. 1:11–12; 5:1; 6:1; 6:16; 7:10–11; 8:1; 11:4–6; 11:20–22; 14:26–33; 15:12.

The Occasion for 1 Corinthians

There are three definite reasons why Paul wrote 1 Corinthians, all of which are indicated in the epistle. First, he had received a report from Chloe's household that there were factions in the congregation (1:11–12). Second, he had received a letter from the congregation in which they asked him several questions (7:1)—at least the questions implied in the sections beginning with the phrase "now concerning" (7:1; 8:1; 12:1; 16:1). The topics of chapters 11 and 15 also may have been replies to questions included in the congregation's letter to Paul. Third, a delegation of three Corinthian Christians (Stephanas, Fortunatus, and Achaicus) arrived when Paul was at Ephesus and informed him about conditions at Corinth

(16:17). They may also have delivered the letter from the congregation.

These three sources of information—the report, the letter, and the delegation—convinced Paul that it was imperative for him to write the church at Corinth immediately. The Corinthian church had problems—problems so serious that we might marvel that Paul still considered them Christians. Factions in the congregation, "incest," people dragging one another into court, people becoming drunk at the Lord's Supper, denial of the resurrection—these are some of the serious evils that had infiltrated the church at Corinth, which had been founded by Paul only a few years earlier.

What would our reaction be today if we were told that a sister congregation was guilty of such serious error? Would we tend to be legalistic or would we approach the situation from an evangelical position? It is most interesting that in spite of the serious problems (or maybe on account of them) Paul adopts a most evangelical approach. After his introductory sentence (1:1–3), Paul states that he thanks God always that the Corinthian Christians are enriched in Christ with all speech and knowledge, are not lacking in any spiritual gift, and will be sustained by Christ until the end, when they will be found guiltless in the day of our Lord Jesus Christ (1:4–9). What an evangelical approach in the face of such serious problems! Paul shows confidence in the power of the Gospel message even in the face of serious error.

The various evils at Corinth stemmed from the rationalistic background of the native Greek culture and its tendency to value human wisdom very highly. The problems are treated by Paul in a firm manner yet with confidence that an evangelical approach is the best way to a solution.

Rival Factions

On the basis of human standards some members preferred the eloquent Apollos as pastor to the tentmaker Paul. Others, who probably had come to Corinth from a place in Judea where Peter (Cephas) had preached, favored allegiance to Peter, since he was one of the original disciples of Jesus. Apparently another group claimed the exclusive right to be labeled Christians, emphasizing the gifts of the Spirit and professing superior knowledge that made them "free" to engage in sexual sins (1:10–17).

Paul tells the Corinthians, who are priding themselves on intellectual superiority and are still bound by the world's way of thinking, that human cleverness is a far cry from God's wisdom (1:18–

2:16). A person must become a fool in the eyes of the world in order to become really wise (3:18). There is no place for pride among Christians or for looking down on others. Christians should regard themselves as God's slaves (chap. 4).

Moral Lapses

Chapters five and six discuss three types of moral lapses. First, the superior knowledge and freedom claimed by some Corinthians resulted in a case of "incest"—a man living with his stepmother, presumably after his father's death. Paul advises expulsion from the congregation if this person does not mend his ways and repent (chap. 5).

Second, Christian brothers were taking each other to civil courts. Even Jews at this time preferred not to take cases before Gentile courts—not because the courts were corrupt, but because they would be admitting their inability to live by their own laws. Paul advises the Christians at Corinth to settle their own internal disputes. It is better to be wronged, Paul advises, than to drag one another into court (6:1–11).

Third, some Corinthian Christians were not abstaining from sexual immorality, as the Apostolic Council had reminded Christians to do (Acts 15:20, 29). At Corinth some felt that they were free to do anything. Sexual needs, like hunger, must be satisfied—even outside of marriage. Paul sternly warns that a Christian, who is a member of the body of Christ, must not join his body to the body of a prostitute (6:12–20).

Questions about Marriage

Chapter seven takes up some questions that the Christians raised about marriage. Several of them reflect the Greek attitude that considered the physical aspect of life inferior to intellectual pursuits and at times even evil. Should married couples continue sexual relations after conversion? Paul says yes (7:1–7). Should single members marry? Paul prefers the single life—provided the individuals have the ability of self-control (7:8–9). May Christians be divorced? Paul answers no (7:10–11). What about the unconverted wife or husband? Paul advises the Christian to remain with the unbelieving mate (7:12–16). He substantiates his advice with the examples of circumcision and slavery (7:17–24). Should engaged couples marry? Paul replies that they may marry, but in those very troubled times single persons may prefer not to marry (7:25–

38). May a widow marry? Paul answers yes, but he believes that she may be happier as a widow (7:39–40).

STUDY QUESTION 4

Christian freedom and its limitations.

A. What principles does Paul lay down in 1 Cor. 8?

B. How do Acts 16:1–3 and Gal. 5:2–4 support the principles of Christian freedom?

Food Offered to Idols

The next three chapters (8–10) concern food offered to heathen gods at the Greek temples. Christians in Corinth at times found it difficult to make a clean break with paganism. Meat sold at temples had previously been sacrificed to idols. It no doubt was cheaper than that at local butcher shops. Could Christians take advantage of these bargains? Some Corinthians believed they had this freedom since the idols represented nonexistent deities. Other Corinthians had scruples and considered eating such food a sin. Paul replies that Christians were free to partake of such food— provided that their free choice did not offend the conscience of fellow Christians who were worried about such a practice.

Public Worship

Chapter 11 takes up two disorders at public worship—one concerned women's veils (11:1–16), the other concerned conduct at the Lord's Supper (11:17–34). At Corinth no decent woman would appear unveiled in public places. Appearing without a veil could be viewed as a sign of moral indecency—similar to the attitude regarding the wearing of rouge and the bobbing of hair at the time of World War I. The veil guaranteed a woman's safety and respect in the streets. The customs of the Greeks and the Jews concerning prayer were also different. Greek women and men prayed with their heads uncovered. Roman and Jewish men and women prayed with their heads covered. Was there a ruling for the church? Paul's answer is based on the place of men and women in their created order. Men, created first, are under Christ's authority alone and should pray bareheaded. Women, created second, are under the husband's authority and should pray veiled. Paul's advice also respects the current social convention in Corinthian society.

In the early church the celebration of the Lord's Supper could take place in connection with a common meal or love feast for members of the congregation. The Christians brought whatever food they could afford, sharing it with each other. Such a practice would demonstrate love for each other and especially for the poor of the congregation. A present comparable practice would be our potluck suppers. In Corinth, however, some members could not wait for everyone to arrive before they began eating and drinking. The result was that some did not get enough to eat, while others had too much to drink. In such a state some of them partook of Holy Communion. Paul tackles this problem by reminding the Corinthians of the circumstances in which Jesus instituted the Lord's Supper and advises serious self-examination before partaking of it.

STUDY QUESTION 5

    A. What spiritual gifts does Paul list in 1 Cor. 12:4–11?

    B. How long does Paul say these gifts are to remain? See 1 Cor. 13:8–13.

    C. What is Paul's advice concerning speaking in tongues? See 1 Cor. 14:1–19; 26–33.

Spiritual Gifts

In chapters 12–14 Paul discusses the matter of spiritual gifts. In Greek religion ecstatic speech indicated a high spiritual status. It was not surprising that the Corinthian Christians coveted especially the gift of "tongues." Paul teaches that this gift is not to be overvalued. Other gifts that are more important for the life of the church should be sought more strenuously. Prophecy, for example, which results in a message from God that everyone can understand, is of more value than "tongues," which needs an interpreter.

Three virtues will outlive all gifts—faith, hope, and love. And love outshines all other gifts. As Paul paints the picture of love in chapter 13, he is drawing a portrait of Jesus Himself. Jesus is the personification of long-suffering and self-giving love. Without Him there would be no church.

STUDY QUESTION 6

The resurrection of the body.

A. How closely does Paul connect Christ's resurrection with our resurrection? See 1 Cor. 15:1–19.

B. Try to explain what is meant by being "baptized for the dead" in 1 Cor. 15:29. Note the practice of the Mormons.

C. How does Paul "explain" the resurrection of the body in 1 Cor. 15:35–58?

Resurrection

Chapter 15 is the classic passage in Scripture on the resurrection from the dead. In Paul's day most of the Jews believed in the resurrection of the body—the same body that had died. The Greeks emphasized the immortality of the soul. A resurrection of the body seemed ridiculous to them, as we see from Paul's speech at Athens (Acts 17:32). Also the Sadducees among the Jews refused to believe in a resurrection (Acts 23:6–8). So it is not surprising that the topic of resurrection should trouble some Christians at Corinth.

Paul explains that Christ's resurrection is of the greatest importance. It is a fact on which Christianity stands or falls, and it is an event well attested, since most of the people who saw the risen Christ about 25 years earlier are still living. Christ's resurrection, moreover, implies and guarantees the resurrection of Christians. The body to be raised, however, will be superior to the body that is buried. The physical and mortal will become spiritual and immortal.

The mention of being "baptized for the dead" (1 Cor. 15:29) does not reflect a practice that Paul is recommending but no doubt refers to a mistaken view of some Corinthians. Paul cites this incorrect practice as evidence that even these people believe in the resurrection of the body—just as the false teaching of Mormons today could be cited as proof that they believe in the resurrection of the body.

1 Corinthians 16

The final chapter gives encouragement for the collection of money for the needy people at Jerusalem. After commenting on a future visit to Corinth, Paul closes with greetings from Christians in Asia (today, western Turkey) and from Aquila and Priscilla in particular, who are hosts to a house church at Ephesus, the capital of the province of Asia.

Outline

I. Disorders reported to Paul (probably by Chloe's people) (1–6)
   A. Factions in the church (1–4)
   B. Moral lapses (5–6)
      1. Case of "incest" (5)
      2. Lawsuits (6:1–11)
      3. Immorality (6:12–20)
II. Questions raised by the Corinthian Christians (probably by letter and delegation) (7–15)
   A. Marriage and celibacy (7)
   B. Food sacrificed to idols (8–10)
   C. Disorders in public worship (11)
      1. Women's dress (11:1–16)
      2. Conduct at the Lord's Supper (11:17–34)
   D. Spiritual gifts (12–14)
   E. Resurrection (15)
III. Conclusion (16)

Once again, what stands out in 1 Corinthians is the danger that the recently founded congregation on Greek soil will slip back into some of their previous habits and the tendency to emphasize human wisdom above divine revelation. Equally noteworthy is Paul's pastoral and evangelical approach to their errors in doctrine and in practice as he meets the problems with confidence in the power of the Gospel as the only basis for solutions.

9. 2 Corinthians: The Effect of the Gospel on Problems at Corinth

Paul's Contacts with Corinth

According to the Acts of the Apostles Paul visited Corinth twice—on his second journey when he founded the congregation (Acts 18:1–18) and on his third journey (Acts 20:1–3). In the time between these two journeys Paul wrote 1 Corinthians and 2 Corinthians. This has been the traditional view concerning Paul's contacts with Corinth.

Currently, however, there is another, more widespread view with which we should be acquainted. Most scholars would outline Paul's contacts with Corinth as follows:

1. Visit on second journey
2. A letter prior to 1 Corinthians
3. 1 Corinthians
4. An intermediate "painful visit" to Corinth
5. An intermediate "sorrowful letter"
6. 2 Corinthians (or part of it)
7. Visit on third journey.

We should make it very clear that we are not dealing with doctrine or matters of faith when we discuss the two views on Paul's contacts with Corinth. Whether we prefer the traditional view or the currently more popular theory makes absolutely no difference in Paul's teaching in relation to the Corinthian congregation. Former professors at Concordia Seminary in St. Louis took different views—my professor, Dr. William Arndt, preferred the traditional theory; his successor, Dr. Martin Franzmann, thought the other more correct.

We are discussing this topic because it is a good example to show how specialists deal with the same evidence and come to different conclusions on historical questions. We shall briefly point to the evidence (the pertinent passages), show the various interpretations of the evidence, and let the reader draw his or her own conclusions.

STUDY QUESTION 1

Did Paul write a letter to Corinth prior to our 1 Corinthians? See 1 Cor. 5:9–11. Note that the verb in Greek for "I wrote" and "I have written" could also be translated "I am writing," as it should be translated in Gal. 6:11.

A Letter Prior to 1 Corinthians

In the last chapter we noted that Paul wrote 1 Corinthians from Ephesus (1 Cor. 16:8) on his third journey. Had he written a previous letter to Corinth or not? The evidence for a previous letter is taken from 1 Corinthians 5:9–11. As indicated above, the Greek verb translated "I wrote" and "I have written" could be rendered "I am writing" or "I write." So this passage could be referring to a previous letter or to the present 1 Corinthians. That the Greek verb could mean "I am writing" or "I write" as well as "I wrote" and "I have written" is clear from Gal. 6:11, which should read: "See with what large letters I am writing to you with my own hand." Paul has just taken the pen (from a public stenographer to whom he had dictated the letter to that point) and is now writing the concluding verses in his own handwriting. His writing is not as neat as that of the stenographer. Here the verb in Greek is in the same tense as the verbs in 1 Cor. 5:9–11.

STUDY QUESTION 2

Did Paul visit Corinth between the writing of 1 Corinthians and 2 Corinthians?

A. *Note Paul's original travel plan in 1 Cor. 16:5–6.*
B. *Note that Paul later considered a change of travel plan in 2 Cor. 1:15–17.*
C. *Did Paul actually carry out the changed plan or not? Note these phrases: "I intended" and "I was planning" (2 Cor. 1:15–17), "I came no more" (2 Cor. 1:23), "the third time I am ready" (2 Cor. 12:14), "the third time . . . as if I were present the second time" (2 Cor. 13:1–2). See also 2 Cor. 2:1.*

An Intermediate Visit

According to 1 Cor. 16:5–6 Paul originally planned to visit Corinth after he left Ephesus and traveled through Macedonia. According to 2 Cor. 1:15–17, however, Paul later considered a change in travel plans—to go from Ephesus to Corinth directly and then to Macedonia and back through Corinth to Judea. The question is whether Paul actually carried out his change in plan. Note that Paul states: "I intended to come to you. . . . I was planning this" (2 Cor. 1:15–17). It is possible that Paul never carried out his change in plan, for later in the same chapter he writes: "To spare you I came no more to Corinth" (2 Cor. 1:23). If Paul considered a change in plan but never carried it out, there would be no evidence in the Corinthian correspondence for an intermediate visit between 1 Corinthians and 2 Corinthians.

Three other passages must be cited in this connection. Toward the end of 2 Corinthians (12:14) Paul asserts: "Now for the third time I am ready to come to you." He is referring to his visit on the third journey (Acts 20:1–3), which according to Acts would be his second visit to Corinth. Here again the evidence may be interpreted in two ways. The phrase "third time" could be stressed and the conclusion would be that Paul did make an intermediate visit, which would have been his second visit to Corinth, according to his changed travel plan. Or one could stress the phrase *"ready to come"* and conclude that he had been *ready* to come but did *not actually* come, in order to spare the Corinthians as he seems to say previously (2 Cor. 1:23).

The beginning of the last chapter of 2 Corinthians is another passage pertinent to Paul's visits to Corinth: "This will be the third time I am coming to you. . . . as if I were present the second time, and now being absent I write . . ." (2 Cor. 13:1–2). This passage may indicate an intermediate visit. That would make the second visit in Acts 20:2–3 actually his third visit, and the intermediate visit would be the second. But again the Greek text is not as specific as it appears in many English translations. The phrase "the third time I am coming to you" could mean "the third time I am going to come" (in the sense of "I am planning to come"). But more important, many translations do not accurately reproduce the Greek when they have "when present on my second visit." The Greek text has a participle ("as being present the second time") and not a temporal clause ("when present on my second visit"). Thus an equally correct translation (interpreting the participle as conditional rather than temporal) would be "as if I were present the second time." That is, Paul is saying that he now is warning the Corinthians, as if he were present the second time, although he is absent in person.

Two interpretations of 2 Corinthians 2:1 are also possible. Paul says: "I would not come again to you in sorrow." Does this sentence refer to a second visit, which Paul did not wish to make while he was in a sorrowful state of mind—that is, "not come again," this time "in sorrow"? Or does it imply that he did not wish to come to Corinth again in sorrow, as if he had previously made an intermediate sorrowful visit? Most translators do not stick strictly to the Greek text but virtually produce commentary by giving the reader only one of the two possible interpretations instead of allowing the reader to make the decision. The usual rendition is as follows: "So I made up my mind that I would not make another painful visit to you" (New International Version). The New King James Version (NKJV), however, leaves the choice to the reader, as it should, by sticking closely to the Greek text: "But I determined this within myself, that I would not come again to you in sorrow." (The fact that it normally follows the Greek text, as in this case, is one of the prime reasons for using the NKJV throughout this volume.)

In brief, the evidence for an intermediate visit is not so clear-cut as some scholars would have us believe. It all depends on how the evidence is interpreted. We must examine the Greek text, for English translations frequently side with one interpretation by their choice of words and grammatical construction.

STUDY QUESTION 3

Did Paul write to Corinth between composing 1 Corinthians and 2 Corinthians?

A. Note that a letter from Paul caused sorrow among the Christians. See 2 Cor. 2:4–11; 7:8–12.

B. May these passages refer to 1 Corinthians or must they refer to an "intermediate letter," written between 1 and 2 Corinthians? Note that a certain person was urged to repent and apparently did so.

An Intermediate Letter

The view that Paul wrote an intermediate letter between 1 Corinthians and 2 Corinthians, which caused sorrow to the church at Corinth, is based primarily on two passages. Paul says: "Out of much affliction and anguish of heart I wrote to you, with many tears. . . . This punishment which was inflicted by the majority is sufficient for such a man, so that, on the contrary, you ought rather to forgive and comfort him. . . . For to this end I also wrote, that I might put you to the test. . . . Now whom you forgive anything, I also forgive" (2 Cor. 2:4–11). "Even if I made you sorry with my letter, I do not regret it; though I did regret it. For I perceive that the same epistle made you sorry, though only for a while. . . . Therefore, although I wrote to you, I did not do it for the sake of him who had done the wrong, nor for the sake of him who suffered wrong, but that our care for you in the sight of God might appear to you" (2 Cor. 7:8, 12).

The crux of these two passages is that Paul wrote a letter to Corinth "with many tears" concerning a person who was in need of repentance. Again the evidence may be interpreted differently. Those who see in these passages references to an intermediate letter also hold to an intermediate visit. They assume that during this visit some member of the congregation offended Paul. Paul then wrote an intermediate letter demanding the punishment of the offender. Other students of Scripture see references to 1 Corinthians in the phrases concerning an offender who is in need of repentance. They assume that several items in 1 Corinthians caused Paul to write "with many tears"—the man involved in "incest" and the people yielding to prostitution, as well as those who were partaking of the Lord's Supper after having imbibed too much wine.

The Integrity of 2 Corinthians

So far the questions concerning a previous letter, an intermediate visit, and an intermediate letter are based on evidence that admits of more than one interpretation. A related question concerns the unity or integrity of 2 Corinthians. Did Paul write 2 Corinthians as we have it, or is our present document a combination of several letters that were later joined by the church? Many who deny the unity of 2 Corinthians wish to see in 2 Corinthians 6:14–7:1 a remnant from a letter written prior to 1 Corinthians. They also frequently regard 2 Cor. 10–13 as part of Paul's intermediate sorrowful letter. In spite of these attempts to chop up 2 Corinthians in this fashion, there is unity in the letter, as we shall note when we discuss its general content and outline.

STUDY QUESTION 4

How do the following passages help to fix the time and place of 2 Corinthians: 2 Cor. 2:12–13; 7:5–7; 8:16–24?

Time and Place

First Corinthians was written, as noted previously, around A.D. 53–54 in Ephesus on Paul's third journey (1 Cor. 16:8). After leaving Ephesus Paul traveled to Troas and then to Macedonia, where Titus met him with a report from Corinth (2 Cor. 2:12–13; 7:5–7). At which city in Macedonia Paul composed 2 Corinthians is not certain. It could have been Philippi, as the subscription at the end of some manuscripts states, or it could have been Thessalonica. The passages cited above, however, do indicate that Paul wrote 2 Corinthians during his third journey and in Macedonia, which he visited between his work at Ephesus and Corinth. The date would be several months after 1 Corinthians, probably in A.D. 54–55. Paul sent 2 Corinthians to Corinth by Titus, who was accompanied by two fellow Christians (2 Cor. 8:16–24).

STUDY QUESTION 5

Note how 2 Corinthians discusses the past in chapters 1–7, the present in chapters 8–9, and the future in chapters 10–13.

114

Content

Second Corinthians is no doubt the most intensely personal of Paul's epistles. In it he shows the weight and burden of his care for all the churches, especially for the congregation at Corinth with its numerous and serious problems. Paul also displays his deep love and anguished concern for their spiritual progress. Furthermore, we see the personal cost of his missionary endeavors—hardship, suffering, humiliation—and his unshakable faith throughout his tribulations.

The personal nature of 2 Corinthians makes it one of the most difficult to analyze. The general threefold division, however, is clear. Paul takes the reader from Ephesus through Troas to Macedonia in the first seven chapters. He lingers for a moment in Macedonia while he treats the topic of the collection for Jerusalem in chapters eight and nine. Then in the last four chapters he considers the conditions in the church at Corinth from the point of view of his coming visit. Thus the three major sections of the epistle treat in order the past with its misunderstandings, the present with its practical collection, and the near future with its anxieties.

Titus had reported some good news. The Corinthians had listened to Paul's advice. They disciplined the offender, who repented, asked for forgiveness, and desired to see Paul again (2 Cor. 2:6; 7:6–16). But there was also a negative side. A minority at Corinth was still maliciously misinterpreting Paul's actions—for example, his change in travel plans (2 Cor. 1:15–17)—and was trying to undermine his apostolic authority. They may have brought the collection for the poor at Jerusalem to a standstill.

Paul's primary purpose in 2 Corinthians is to explain and defend his apostolic authority. At the same time he takes the opportunity to encourage the continuation of the collection for Jerusalem. It is in the last section of the epistle that he deals with those who are still opposing him.

Paul's critics attacked him on several points. They regarded him as a good writer of letters but inferior when met face to face (10:1, 9–11) and as a second-rate apostle, since he insists on earning his own livelihood (11:5–7). Paul replies that when he arrives, the critics will find him as ready to act as to write (10:1–11), and that apostleship does not consist in oratory (11:6). He earned his own livelihood because he did not wish to burden them financially (11:7–15).

STUDY QUESTION 6

How does Paul "boast" in defending his apostleship in 2 Cor. 11:1–12:18?

One of the most beautiful passages in 2 Corinthians is Paul's extended "boasting" in defense of his career as an apostle (11:1–12:18). In the passage he lists his various trials (beatings, imprisonments, shipwrecks), his vision of Christ 14 years earlier, and his "thorn in the flesh." Not all of these experiences are recorded by Luke in Acts, for Luke had to be selective in choosing his material in order to keep the document within the limits of one scroll.

Finally, 2 Corinthians is valuable in that it illustrates how Paul continued to apply the Gospel to the problems at Corinth and how such an application in 1 Corinthians had a salutary effect on the congregation, leading it, as we see in 2 Corinthians, to several God-pleasing solutions. Also today the Gospel is our sole means of building the church—both in outward expansion and in inward growth and maturity.

Outline

10. Romans: Gospel of God's Grace as a Missionary Platform

STUDY QUESTION 1

What kind of people were members of the church at Rome? See Rom. 4:1; 9:10; 16:7; 7:1–6; see also Rom. 1:13; 11:13; 15:16. See Acts 2:10.

Rome was the capital of an empire that extended from Britain to Arabia. Since it was the political and commercial center of the Mediterranean world, Rome was wealthy and cosmopolitan. The current peace (*Pax Romana*) and extensive roads throughout the empire made travel safe and easy. Rome was the largest city of that time. Estimates of its population usually range from one to two million, with one estimate as high as four million on the basis of inscriptions found at Ostia, the harbor at the mouth of the Tiber River. Rome itself was on the Tiber about 15 miles inland.

There was a large Jewish community in Rome after 63 B.C., when Pompey captured Jerusalem and brought captives to Rome. Some scholars see evidence for at least 11 Jewish synagogues in Rome, which no doubt gradually attracted many Gentile converts to Judaism. That the church at Rome consisted of both Jews and Gentiles is evident from several passages. Paul's references to "Abraham, our father" (4:1), "our father Isaac" (9:10), and "my kinsmen" (16:7) and to the contrast between a previous state under Jewish law and a state of freedom (7:1–6) indicate a Jewish membership in the church in Rome. Other references, however, clearly point to a large Gentile membership. Paul states that he desired to visit the Roman Christians "that I might have some fruit among you also, just as among the other Gentiles" (1:13). He also writes: "For I speak to you Gentiles" (11:13) and claims to be addressing them as a "minister of Jesus Christ to the Gentiles" (15:16).

The Origin of the Church

We have no definite information on the origin of the church at Rome. Of the churches considered previously—Galatia, Thessalonica, Corinth—we know that Paul was the founder, as is clear from his epistles to these congregations and from the Acts of the Apostles. But in respect to Rome we are left to speculate.

One possible origin—even a very probable origin—is from Pentecost, at which occasion there were "visitors from Rome, both Jews and proselytes" (Acts 2:10). It is very likely that some or most of these people were converted at Pentecost and began a Christian congregation at Rome on their return. But it is also claimed by some scholars that these "visitors" at Pentecost were foreign-born Jews who had taken up residence at Jerusalem in their old age in order to die and be buried on Jewish soil. In this case those "from Rome" would not be returning to Rome to found a church there.

Another possibility proposed by scholars is that various converts of Paul in the eastern Mediterranean found their way to Rome, the capital of the empire, and began a Christian congregation. Or Christians in general from Judea, Asia, Greece, and Macedonia (whether or not converted by Paul) may have traveled to Rome and spread the Gospel. It is also possible that the church at Rome was begun by the soldiers from Italy who were stationed at Caesarea with Cornelius (Acts 10:1) and who then were converted by Peter and later returned to Rome and founded a church. In the final analysis, the origin of the church at Rome stemming from Pentecost seems to be the most likely.

There are two people, however, to whom we should not credit the origin of the church at Rome. A later tradition has Peter as the founder of the church at Rome and claims that he worked there for about 25 years before his death. This tradition should not be accepted, since it would put Peter in Rome soon after A.D. 40, and we know from Acts 15 that Peter was still in Jerusalem in A.D. 49 for the Apostolic Council. It is true, however, that Peter later did live in Rome (1 Pet. 5:13, where "Babylon" stands for Rome) and according to tradition suffered martyrdom there.

The other person to whom we should not credit the origin of the church at Rome is Paul, for both Paul's Epistle to the Romans and the Acts of the Apostles make the point clear. In Romans Paul specifically states that he had intended to come to Rome but so far was prevented from making the journey (Rom. 1:10–13; 15:22) and that he had preached from Jerusalem to Illyricum (15:19). Acts gives a connected account of Paul's travels, but his arrival at Rome does not occur until the last chapter (Acts 28:14–16) after his two-year imprisonment at Caesarea. The fact that the faith of the Roman Christians "is spoken of throughout the whole world" (Rom. 1:8) indicates that the founding of their church must have occurred some years earlier, long before Paul ever arrived at Rome.

STUDY QUESTION 2

What evidence do we have for the time and place of Paul's Letter to the Romans?

A. For the time see Rom. 15:25–28; 1 Cor. 16:1–4; Acts 24:17.

B. For the place see Acts 20:1–3; 1 Cor. 16:6; Rom. 16:1; 16:23; 1 Cor. 1:14; 2 Tim. 4:20.

Time and Place

Evidence for the time and place of the writing of Romans is found in various documents of the New Testament. Paul tells the Romans that although he has never visited them, he hopes to see them in the future. He has just raised a collection for the Christians in Jerusalem, which he is going to deliver (Rom. 15:25–26), and then he plans to visit Rome on his way to Spain (Rom. 15:28). Paul speaks of this collection also in his letters to Corinth (1 Cor. 16:1–4; 2 Cor. 8 and 9), composed on his third journey. Furthermore, when he speaks before Felix, Paul refers to the collection for Jerusalem (Acts 24:17), delivered at the end of his third journey. All of this evidence places the composition of Romans toward the end of Paul's third journey.

Concerning the place of composition all the evidence points to Corinth. Acts 20:1–3 tells us that toward the end of his third journey Paul spent three months in Greece. This information agrees with Paul's promise to the Corinthians that he would stay with them "or even spend the winter" with them after he passed through Macedonia (1 Cor. 16:6). The evidence from Romans also points to the same conclusion—that Paul wrote Romans while he was in Corinth on his third journey. He asks the Christians at Rome to receive Phoebe, a deaconess of the church at Cenchrea, who is probably the bearer of Paul's Epistle to the Romans (Rom. 16:1). Since Cenchrea is an eastern harbor of Corinth, it seems that Paul wrote from Corinth. Furthermore Paul writes: "Gaius, my host and the host of the whole church, greets you" (Rom. 16:23). That is, Paul is a guest at the home of Gaius, who was a member of the church at Corinth (1 Cor. 1:14). Paul sends greetings also from Erastus, the city treasurer (Rom. 16:23). Erastus is mentioned in another letter as being in Corinth (2 Tim. 4:20). An inscription found at Corinth, moreover, mentions a city official by the name of Erastus.

The evidence then points to the writing of Romans on the third missionary journey at Corinth, where Paul planned to spend the winter. Thus Paul's three longest epistles were composed during the third journey—1 Corinthians from Ephesus, 2 Corinthians from Macedonia, and Romans from Corinth. According to the chronology that we are following, the time would be the winter months of A.D. 55–56. This conclusion would agree with Phoebe's plan to travel from Corinth to Rome (Rom. 16:1–2). Since navigation on the Mediterranean Sea frequently was avoided from around November 10 to March 10, it would seem that the Epistle to the Romans was written during January or February, with its delivery through Phoebe around the middle of March.

The evidence from Acts points to the same conclusion. Originally Paul had hoped to go directly to Jerusalem from Corinth to deliver the collection (Rom. 15:25). But a plot against him by the Jews forced him to change his plan and to go to Jerusalem by way of Macedonia (Acts 20:3). He left Philippi, a city in Macedonia, "after the Days of Unleavened Bread" (Acts 20:6)—that is, after the Easter season. The conclusion based on this evidence is that Paul probably wrote Romans in January-February of A.D. 56 before he discovered the plot against him. On discovery of the plot, he traveled north by land and left Philippi a few weeks after he departed from Corinth. We must repeat, however, as mentioned in a previous chapter, that this chronology is a close approximation; the actual dates may vary a year or so either way.

STUDY QUESTION 3

Why did Paul write Romans?

A. *See Rom. 15:24 and 28; compare Rom. 15:20; 1:8; 16:19.*

B. *The Greek verb for "to be helped on" in Rom. 15:24 also occurs in Acts 15:3; 20:38; 21:5; 1 Cor. 16:6, 11; 2 Cor. 1:16; Titus 3:13; and 3 John 6. Note that this verb seems to refer to moral and financial support of missionary work.*

C. *How does a missionary purpose for Romans explain its detailed treatment of doctrine?*

The Occasion for Romans

The immediate occasion for writing to the Roman Christians is clear from the letter itself—to prepare them for Paul's visit, which he expects will be soon. What this immediate occasion involves, however, implies several factors.

Since Rome is not his final goal but merely a stopover on his way to Spain (Rom. 15:24, 28), the missionary aspect of Romans is Paul's primary purpose. His policy was not to preach the Gospel where it had already been preached and not to "build on another man's foundation" (15:20). The foundation had already been built in Rome, for the faith of its believers was proclaimed throughout the world (1:8), and their obedience was known to all (16:19). As noted earlier, the Christian church at Rome probably dated back to Pentecost. Paul planned to spend time in Rome and "to be helped on" by the Romans on his journey to Spain (15:24, 28).

The phrase "to be helped on" may serve as a clue to the missionary aspect of Romans. In all of its occurrences in the New Testament (Rom. 15:24; Acts 15:3; 20:38; 21:5; 1 Cor. 16:6, 11; 2 Cor. 1:16; Titus 3:13; 3 John 6) the phrase seems to be a technical expression for moral and financial support of missionary work from established churches or individual Christians. Paul expects the Roman Christians to be of assistance in his proposed missionary trip to Spain. He wishes Rome to be the base for his missionary work in the western Mediterranean as Antioch of Syria had been his base for his three journeys in the eastern Mediterranean. Paul and Barnabas had worked at Antioch for a full year before beginning missionary journeys (Acts 11:26). But now close to 60 years of age, Paul feels that he does not have the time to spend a long period in Rome. So his Epistle to the Romans and a brief visit must accomplish what a year's ministry achieved in Antioch.

This missionary aspect of Romans, written in preparation for Paul's visit to Rome, explains its length and depth. He wishes the Roman Christians, as his base for missionary work in Spain, to have a thorough understanding of the Gospel message. The church at Rome may have heard slanderous misrepresentations of his preaching. If so, this misinformation must be corrected. He must also make it clear that his missionary journeys are to emphasize true doctrine and not any social gospel.

Another factor in the purpose of Romans concerns the history of the congregation and the implication of the Gospel. As we have noted earlier, the church at Rome originally consisted primarily of Jewish Christians; later a large number of Gentile converts became members. If Paul wishes to win the church at Rome as the base for his missionary work, he must be sure that the Roman Christians understand the relation between Jew and Gentile as set forth in the Gospel. No doubt Paul's journey to Jerusalem with the collection from his Gentile churches was prompted to a large extent by his desire to bring these two groups into mutual respect and understanding. So he goes to great lengths in Romans to prove that the Gospel is for both Jew and Gentile and is able to unite them into one church. His presentation of the universal Gospel should strengthen the faith of the Roman Christians and prepare them to assist in supporting him in his missionary endeavors.

In this connection it is possible to assume that there may have been a current problem at Rome. We know that Aquila and Priscilla came from there in A.D. 49 because the Roman emperor Claudius had expelled the Jews from Rome (Acts 18:1–2). At this time the church at Rome apparently was trying to evangelize the Jewish quarter. This effort no doubt stirred up unrest. A Roman biographer, Suetonius, states that Claudius expelled the Jews who were boisterous or riotous (*tumultantes* in Latin), the point of contention being a person by the name of Chrestus (of course, a misunderstanding of Christus, the Latin name for Christ). With the expulsion of Jewish leaders, Gentile Christians took over control of the church. Since the expulsion remained in effect only as long as the emperor was alive, and since Claudius died in A.D. 54, Jewish Christians could then return to Rome, as Aquila and Priscilla actually did (Rom. 16:3–4). These returning Jewish Christians probably noticed changes in the church as a result of Gentile leadership. The relief of this tension could have been a factor in Paul's mind in composing his Epistle to the Romans.

Other factors, though more minor, also may have been on Paul's mind as he wrote Romans. He planned to visit Jerusalem before his trip to Rome. A passage in Romans indicates that he had some misgivings concerning the outcome of that journey—a journey that actually led to a riot at Jerusalem, two years of imprisonment at Caesarea, and two years of house arrest at Rome. So Paul appeals to the Roman Christians to pray that he "may be delivered from those in Judea who do not believe" and that his "service for Jerusalem may be acceptable to the saints" (Rom. 15:30–33).

Since Paul composed Romans at Corinth, he no doubt also had in mind the errors that had crept into that church. Thinking particularly of the factions at Corinth and the weak consciences of some members concerning practical problems, Paul includes reminders about the weak (Rom. 14) and about any who might create dissensions at Rome (Rom. 16:17–20).

STUDY QUESTION 4

The first large division of Romans discusses justification (1:18–4:25) and is subdivided into two parts.

A. *What is the topic of the first part, 1:18–3:20? Note especially 1:18; 3:10–12; 3:20.*

B. *What is the topic of the second part, 3:21–4:25? Note especially 3:21–24; 3:28.*

C. *What does chapter 4 state about Abraham?*

Content

Paul develops the argument of Romans in a logical manner. He states the theme of the epistle (after his usual introduction) as follows: "I am not ashamed of the Gospel of Christ, for it is the power of God to salvation for everyone who believes, for the Jew first and also for the Greek. For in it the righteousness of God is revealed from faith to faith; as it is written, 'The just shall live by faith' " (Rom. 1:16–17). Paul develops his argument from this quotation. The first four chapters show that righteousness can come only through faith, not by works of the law. The next four chapters (5–8) reveal that a person who is justified through faith will live in freedom from God's wrath (5), from sin (6), from the Law (7), and from death (8). Paul inserts a discussion of Israel's unbelief (9–11) and then discusses the ethics of a person justified through faith (12–14).

Paul's argument in the first four chapters may not be very easy to follow on first reading. We should, therefore, analyze it carefully. Before someone becomes interested in purchasing a household item (a refrigerator, for example) that person must be convinced of a need for it. Likewise, before the readers will listen to Paul's description of God's righteousness, Paul must convince them of their need for it. So he begins, after announcing the theme (1:16–17), with a discussion of God's wrath, which condemns both non-Jews (1:18–32) and Jews (2:1–3:20). All human beings are under the wrath of God by nature and doomed to eternal perdition. Paul charges:

> There is none righteous, no, not one;
> There is none who understands;
> There is none who seeks after God.
> They have all gone out of the way;
> They have together become unprofitable;
> There is none who does good, no, not one. (3:10–12)

He concludes: "Therefore by the deeds of the law no flesh will be justified in His sight, for by the law is the knowledge of sin" (3:20).

Now the readers are prepared to hear of God's righteousness through faith, since any attempted righteousness through deeds of the law leads to God's wrath and damnation. Paul emphatically declares: "But now the righteousness of God apart from the law is revealed . . . even the righteousness of God which is through faith in Jesus Christ to all and on all who believe. For there is no difference; for all have sinned and fall short of the glory of God, being justified freely by his grace through the redemption that is in Christ Jesus" (3:21–24). "Therefore we conclude that a man is justified by faith apart from the deeds of the law" (3:28).

As an example of God's righteousness through faith, Paul in chapter four cites the case of Abraham, the father of the Jewish nation. Scripture states: "Abraham believed God, and it was accounted to him for righteousness" (4:3). That is, God accepted Abraham because of his faith, not because of any good works. Abraham, for example, was reckoned as righteous before he was circumcised, so his submission to circumcision did not contribute to any righteousness. Abraham received righteousness from God because of a promise God made to him, a promise that he accepted through faith. As Abraham is the physical father or forefather of the Jewish people, he is also the spiritual father of all people who are righteous before God as a result of faith. We—Jews and Gentiles—must be people of faith, as Abraham was, trusting in what God has promised us through His Son, Jesus, not relying on what we do. It was Jesus who suffered God's wrath for us. His resurrection assures us that we are justified through faith in Christ.

STUDY QUESTION 5

There are three other large divisions in Romans.
A. What does Paul discuss in chapters 5–8?
B. What is the topic of chapters 9–11?
C. Summarize briefly chapters 12–14.

Chapters 5–8 enlarge on the words "shall live," quoted from Hab. 2:4 in the theme of Romans (1:16–17). Paul interprets the citation as follows: "He who through faith is righteous shall live." These chapters teach that Christians who partake of God's righteousness through faith in Christ *shall live in freedom.* Through the death and resurrection of Jesus, Christians have a life of peace—peace from the wrath of God. Sin began with Adam and spread to all his descendants. Jesus obtained pardon for all and a new life for Christians (chap. 5).

Should Christians continue in sin so that God's grace may abound all the more? By no means! Christians identify themselves with Christ, sharing in His death and resurrection. Although dead to God previously, Christians have a new determination to fight the tug of sin. Serving sin is death; serving God is life, a life transformed by God in us (chap. 6).

Christians realize the limitations of the Law. They no longer try to win God's favor by keeping the Law to the letter. The Law serves its purpose when it causes us to despair of our own efforts and makes us ready to accept what Christ has accomplished for us, when we realize what we cannot do for ourselves (chap. 7).

The Holy Spirit is present and active in Christians. Life in the Spirit is life with a blessed future. The Spirit assures Christians that their mortal bodies will be raised from death. The glory of Christians in eternity will be so great that any suffering in this life cannot outweigh it. In fact, nothing—death, life, angels, principalities, things present, things to come, powers, height, depth—will be able to separate Christians from the love of God in Christ Jesus (chap. 8).

Chapters 9–11 speak of the nation of Israel. God has not broken His word to Israel. Only through God's patience and mercy has a remnant of rebellious Israel survived God's judgment. The fact that Paul and some fellow Jews became Christians proves his point. Gentiles should not disparage the Jews, for in time all Israel—Christians from among both Gentiles and Jews—will be saved.

In chapters 12–14 Paul discusses Christian ethics or the life of those who through faith are righteous. In their relationships to each other, Christians should pool their individual gifts for the benefit of the Christian community. Instead of "getting even" when wronged, Christians are to show love to their enemies (chap. 12). They also should respect the power of civic authorities, since government has been instituted by God. They are to pay taxes and obey the laws (chap. 13). The consciences of Christians may differ on food sacrificed to pagan idols and on Jewish food laws. As Jesus showed love to Christians, so Christians should show love to each other by limiting their freedom rather than offending the conscience of a weak Christian (chap. 14).

Paul concludes the epistle by writing of his travel plans in chapter 15 and by sending greetings and a warning in chapter 16. No doubt Tertius (16:22) was the Christian whom Paul used as a scribe in writing Romans.

STUDY QUESTION 6

How could Paul know so many people (see chapter 16) in a congregation that he had not visited?

Integrity

Some scholars believe that chapter 16 was not part of the original letter to the Romans but probably was addressed to the church at Ephesus. Their arguments are: (1) The benediction at the end of chapter 15 may be the close of the Epistle to the Romans. (2) The doxology (16:25–27) is found at different places in some early manuscripts—at the end of chapter 14 or at the end of chapter 15, for example. (3) The mention of 26 acquaintances at Rome seems unlikely since Paul had never visited there. (4) The frequent change of residence by Aquila and Priscilla—Rome to Corinth (Acts 18:1) to Ephesus (Acts 18:18–19) to Rome (Rom. 16:3–5) and back to Ephesus (1 Tim. 1:3 and 2 Tim. 4:19). (5) The warning in 16:17–20 seems too abrupt for the conditions in Rome.

But these arguments are easily answered. (1) A list of greetings is more likely as a lengthy postscript than as a separate letter. (2) The different positions of the doxology merely point to the varying liturgical practices in the different churches, some of which did not read the last chapter or the two final chapters in their churches. (3) These 26 acquaintances could have been known to Paul through their travels, as in the case of Aquila and Priscilla. In only one other epistle to a congregation does Paul mention greetings to any individuals, namely, in Colossians. And he had not visited Colossae before writing to these Christians. Paul was not tactless. In a letter to a church he had founded or visited, sending greetings to some and omitting the names of others would have caused hard feelings on the part of those not mentioned. Sending of greetings to individuals, therefore, seems to fit Rome better than Ephesus. (4) Aquila and Priscilla evidently did a lot of traveling both for the sake of their business interests and to assist Paul in preparation for his visit to Rome, as they had done at Ephesus. (5) The warning in Romans 16:17–20 seems abrupt, but the tone is no more brusque than the numerous imperatives in the preceding four chapters. Finally, and most important, there is no single manuscript or early translation of Romans that separates the last chapter from the rest of this epistle.

The Value of Romans

While it is true that *all* Scripture is inspired by God and profitable for doctrine, reproof, correction, and instruction in righteousness, as St. Paul clearly states (2 Tim. 3:16), it may not be amiss to mention the high value Luther placed particularly on Romans. He writes in his preface:

> This epistle is the very heart and center of the New Testament and the purest and clearest Gospel. It well deserves to be memorized word for word by every Christian. . . . Thus we find in the epistle all that a Christian ought to know, and that in great

abundance, namely, what the Law is, what the Gospel is, what sin and punishment are, what grace, faith, righteousness, Christ, God, good works, love, hope, and the cross are, and what our attitude toward all men ought to be, toward saints and sinners, the strong and the weak, friend and foe, and toward ourselves.

Romans is also extremely valuable and important as a guide and warning in reference to missionary work. For it reminds the church that the content of missionary preaching is of critical importance and must be based on sound doctrine, not on sentimental humanitarian goals.

Outline

Theme: He who through faith is righteous shall live (1:16–17).

I. Introduction (1:1–15)

II. Justification: He who through faith is righteous (1:18–4:25)
- A. Wrath of God (1:18–3:20)
  1. Against the Gentiles (1:18–32)
  2. Against the Jews (2:1–3:20)
- B. Righteousness of God (3:21–4:25)
  1. Through faith, not law (3:21–31)
  2. Example of Abraham (4:1–25)

III. Christian freedom: He . . . shall live (5–8)
- A. Freedom from God's wrath (5)
- B. Freedom from sin (6)
- C. Freedom from the Law (7)
- D. Freedom from death (8)

IV. Israel's unbelief: The righteousness of faith is not against the promise of God (9–11)

V. Ethics: The life of one who through faith is righteous(12–14)

VI. Conclusion (15–16)
- A. Paul's travel plans (15)
- B. Greetings, warning, doxology (16)

11. *Philippians and Philemon: Letters from Prison*

STUDY QUESTION 1

The time and place for the writing of Philippians and Philemon.

A. What was Paul's situation when he wrote these letters? See Philippians 1:7, 13 and Philemon 1, 9, 10, 13, 23.

B. How do Acts 19:1–20:1 and 28:16 seem to indicate that Paul was in this situation in Rome?

C. How may 1 Cor. 15:32; 2 Cor. 1:8; Rom. 16:3–4; Acts 20:19; and 1 Cor. 16:8–9 indicate that this could have been his situation at Ephesus? Compare Rom. 15:24–28 with Philemon 22.

Time and Place

There are four letters, frequently called Captivity Letters, in which Paul refers to himself as a prisoner of Christ Jesus or refers to his chains: Philippians (1:7, 13), Philemon (1, 9, 10, 13, 23), Colossians (4:3, 10, 18), and Ephesians (3:1; 4:1; 6:20). Most scholars view these four epistles as having been written in Rome during Paul's first Roman imprisonment around A.D. 60. Throughout the centuries some students of Scripture have preferred to place the writing of these letters during Paul's imprisonment at Caesarea about A.D. 58. During the 20th century a third opinion has appeared—that Paul wrote all or some of these letters when he was imprisoned at Ephesus, although Acts does not record an imprisonment at Ephesus.

Although no theological teachings are at issue, it may be of interest to mention the main arguments for an origin of these epistles at Ephesus. Paul tells the Corinthians that he was in prison often (2 Cor. 11:23); yet at this point in Paul's career Acts has recorded only one overnight stay in jail—at Philippi. That is, Acts must not be including everything that happened to Paul. Certainly more happened to Paul during his stay of three years at Ephesus than what is reported in Acts (19:1–20:1; 20:31), all of which could have taken place within a few weeks.

In writing to the Corinthians Paul states that he "fought with beasts at Ephesus" (1 Cor. 15:32)—to which no reference is made in Acts—and he speaks of the "trouble which came to us in Asia . . . so that we despaired even of life" (2 Cor. 1:8). In writing to the Romans he refers to Priscilla and Aquila, who assisted him in Ephesus, as "fellow workers in Christ Jesus, who risked their own necks for my life" (Rom. 16:3–4). In addressing the elders from Ephesus he recalls "the plotting of the Jews" (Acts 20:19). In writing to Corinth from Ephesus he mentions that there are "many adversaries" at Ephesus (1 Cor. 16:8–9).

In the opinion of some scholars the historical background in Philippians also points to Ephesus as the place of composition. News of Paul's imprisonment had reached Philippi. The church there sent a gift to Paul, delivered by Epaphroditus. Epaphroditus became ill. News of his illness reached the Philippians, who became worried about his health. News of the concern of the Philippians reached Paul. Such interaction between the Philippian church and Paul, so it is argued, would fit better if Paul were a prisoner at Ephesus rather than at Rome, for the time required for this interchange would be considerably less.

In the opinion of these scholars the historical situation in Paul's Letter to Philemon likewise points to Ephesus as the place of composition. Onesimus, a runaway slave from Colossae, has come into contact with Paul during his imprisonment and has been converted to Christianity by Paul. Paul has convinced Onesimus to return to his master, Philemon, at Colossae. To ensure a favorable reception of Onesimus by Philemon, Paul pens a brief letter, in which he states his plan to visit Philemon as soon as he is released from prison (Philemon 22). Several facts, it is argued, must be kept in mind. The flight of Onesimus from Colossae to *Ephesus*—a distance of about 100 miles—and a visit of Paul from *Ephesus* would have been simpler than if the flight and the visit had involved *Rome* and Colossae. Paul had also expressed plans to travel west to Spain after he had been at Rome (Rom. 15:24–28). A visit to Colossae from *Rome* would have caused a long delay in carrying out his intended missionary work in Spain.

This brief survey on the time and place of the Captivity Letters has only historical interest. Whatever choice a person prefers—Rome, Ephesus, or even Caesarea—does not affect doctrinal issues. It is also possible to separate these four epistles in time and place. Some scholars, for example, place Philippians at Ephesus and Philemon, Colossians, and Ephesians at Rome. It would not seem logical to separate the last three from one another, since Tychicus delivered all three (Eph 6:21–22; Col. 4:7–9).

STUDY QUESTION 2

The church at Philippi. Read Acts 16:12–40.

A. How does Acts 16:12–13 indicate that only a few Jews lived at Philippi?

B. With which three individuals at Philippi did Paul have contact?

C. How did the Philippians show their gratitude? How often did this happen? See Phil. 4:16; 4:15 and 2 Cor. 11:8–9; Phil. 4:18.

D. How does Epaphroditus fit into the picture? See Phil. 4:18; 2:25–30.

Philippi

Philippi, named after Philip II of Macedonia, the father of Alexander the Great, was a Roman colony—as described by Luke (Acts 16:12). Its citizens were Roman citizens on a level with those of Roman colonies in Italy. It was situated on the Egnatian Way, the great northern east-west highway in Macedonia. The population was mixed. Roman colonists were the dominant and ruling class, while the old Macedonian stock was numerically the largest element. Another group consisted of a mixture of Orientals. Since Philippi was more a military and agricultural than a commercial city, few Jews settled there—not enough to have a regular synagogue. Instead, they met at a place of prayer outside the city by the riverside (Acts 16:13). A minimum of 10 men was required to organize a synagogue—a number that Philippi apparently did not have. At Philippi and in the rest of Macedonia women seemed to have enjoyed high social status.

The Origin of the Church

Paul organizes a Christian church at Philippi on his second journey about A.D. 50. It is the first church founded by Paul in Europe. After revisiting the congregations in Galatia with Silas and Timothy, he travels to Troas and receives a call to go to Macedonia. At Troas Luke joins Paul and his company for the trip to Philippi, where Luke apparently remains after Paul leaves. Philippi may have been Luke's hometown. Later, on the return phase of the third journey, Luke again joins Paul on his trip to Jerusalem.

According to Luke's account in Acts 16:12–40, the church at Philippi was begun primarily through Paul's contact with three individuals. One was Lydia, a business woman from the city of Thyatira, who dealt in purple cloth. Another was a slave girl. The third was a jailer.

The activity of Lydia is in accordance with the general high social status of women in the province of Macedonia. In his epistle Paul also mentions two other women who assisted him in spreading the Gospel (Phil. 4:2–3).

The hospitality of Lydia (Acts 16:15) is indicative also of the generosity of the church at Philippi toward Paul throughout his travels. Soon after he left Philippi and went to Thessalonica, the Philippians sent him a financial contribution "once and again" (Phil. 4:16). Later, when Paul was at Corinth, the Philippians sent him another contribution (Phil. 4:15; 2 Cor. 11:8–9). Then shortly before Paul wrote to the Philippians—either from Ephesus on his third journey or from Rome—he again received a contribution from Philippi (Phil. 4:18). In fact, to thank them for this contribution is one of the reasons Paul wrote his Epistle to the Philippians.

STUDY QUESTION 3

Why did Paul write Philippians?

A. *What reason is indicated in Phil. 4:18?*

B. *What reason is indicated in Phil. 1:29–30?*

C. What other reasons are indicated in chapter 3? Note that one group is discussed in 3:1–16 and another in 3:17–21.

The Occasion for Philippians

Epaphroditus had come to Paul with a gift (4:18) and no doubt to report on the general conditions of the church at Philippi. Apparently he was to remain with Paul for a while to assist him in his "need" (2:25)—no doubt referring to his imprisonment. Paul writes that Epaphroditus nearly died in supporting the work of Christ, risking his life "to supply what was lacking in your service toward me" (2:30). The report of Epaphroditus's illness reached Philippi, and news of their concern for him came to Paul (2:26). Now that Epaphroditus has recovered, Paul is sending him back to Philippi with this letter (2:25).

It is interesting to note that the opening sentence states that Paul and Timothy are writing to the saints at Philippi with their bishops and deacons (1:1). Paul mentions Timothy as being with him at the time of writing because Timothy was with Paul when Paul founded the church at Philippi. Paul includes "the bishops and deacons" among the addressees because these "overseers" and "administrators" were no doubt instrumental in collecting and forwarding the financial gift delivered by Epaphroditus. Philippians is the only epistle by Paul that gives special mention to these officers of a congregation in the opening sentence. He does so here because he wishes to acknowledge his indebtedness to them for their part in the financial assistance he received from Philippi.

One of the primary purposes in writing the letter concerns the situation at Philippi, apparently as reported by Epaphroditus. The Philippians are suffering conflict or persecution (1:29–30), and Paul encourages them to be steadfast in the faith. But more important, there is a danger that they will be influenced by two types of false teachers: legalistic Judaizers and antinomian libertines. The former group insisted that Christians must be circumcised and must keep the Old Testament ceremonial law. Paul refutes them in the first part of chapter three (3:1–16). The other group, attacked by Paul in the same chapter (3:17–21), thought that Christians had freedom or liberty to live as worldly people (libertines), assuming that they were above the moral law (antinomian) and setting their minds on earthly things.

It is not certain from Paul's Epistle to the Philippians that the views of these two groups of false teachers had greatly permeated the church at Philippi. Paul may be mainly warning the members of the church because similar teachings had infiltrated other congregations—Judaizers in Galatia and libertines or antinomians at Corinth.

Content of Philippians

The first two chapters review Paul's relationship with the Philippians and supply information about his circumstances. He informs them of the generally satisfactory outcome of his imprisonment (1:12–20), promising to send Timothy as soon as the verdict is known—a verdict that he trusts will be favorable (2:19–24). Chapter two contains a beautiful poetic passage about Jesus Christ (vv. 5–11), which scholars regard as a hymn either quoted by Paul or composed by him. He encourages the Philippians to cultivate unity for their common good with a spirit of humility (1:27–2:4) as exemplified in Christ (2:5–11). And he informs the readers of his plan to send Timothy and Epaphroditus to them (2:19–30).

Chapter three contains a warning against two serious errors that had crept into other churches, if not into Philippi as yet—legalistic Judaism (3:1–16) and antinomianism (3:17–21).

Chapter four begins with various exhortations. Paul appeals for unity between two women, Euodia and Syntyche, showing tact by not mentioning the reason for their disagreement (4:2–3). He then exhorts the Christians to holy living (4:4–7) and to meditation and action (4:8–9). In the latter part of chapter four he expresses his gratitude for the gift sent to him by the Philippians recently, thanking them also for previous gifts (4:10–20).

We should note also that in writing to Philippi, which was a Roman colony, Paul uses several pertinent metaphors. He reminds the Philippians that "our citizenship is in heaven" (3:20). The possession of Roman citizenship meant a great deal to the inhabitants of a Roman colony who enjoyed such a privilege. Paul advises them to regard themselves as a colony of heaven with citizenship in God's kingdom. The Philippians, proud of their status as a Roman colony, would quickly grasp the point of Paul's metaphor.

Another metaphor refers to a military unit first used by Macedonian armies. We call this unit the phalanx—ranks of heavily armed infantry in close and deep formation. The success of such a military unit depended on the closest cooperation of all members of the unit. The people of Philippi, a city in Macedonia, would quickly get the point when Paul advises them to "stand fast in one spirit, with one mind striving together [in the Greek, "side by side"] for the faith of the gospel, and not in any way terrified by your adversaries'' (1:27–28). Paul returns to this military metaphor when he advises them to "stand fast in the Lord" (4:1) and recalls that the two women "have labored [in the Greek, "side by side"] with me" (4:3).

Some scholars also see a play on words in the name of Epaphroditus, but this comparison may be a little farfetched. The name Ep-aphroditus, according to some authorities, may mean "dedicated to Aphrodite," who was the patron goddess of gamblers among the Greeks. These scholars further recall that the highest cast of the dice was called an *epaphroditus,* because the goddess was credited with directing the hand that threw the dice. It is claimed that Paul is adopting a gambling metaphor when he describes the service of Epaphroditus: "For the work of Christ he came close to death, *risking his life* [according to most manuscripts] to supply what was lacking in your service toward me" (2:30). The implication of "risking" would be that Epaphroditus had gambled with his life and won because God was with him.

Outline of Philippians

    I. Introduction: Greeting and prayer (1:1–11)
    II. Personal news (1:12–26)
    III. Plea for unity (1:27–2:18)
    IV. Commending of fellow workers (2:19–20)
    V. Warning against false teachers (3:1–21)
    VI. Further exhortations (4:1–9)
    VII. Thanks for gifts (4:10–20)
    VIII. Conclusion: Greetings (4:21–23)

STUDY QUESTION 4

Reconstruct the background of Paul's Letter to Philemon.

A. **What had Onesimus done? See vv. 15–16, 18.**
B. **What was Paul's relationship to Onesimus? See v. 10.**
C. **What was Paul's relationship to Philemon? See v. 19.**

D. *The name "Onesimus" means "useful" or "prof-*
   itable" or "beneficial." Now read vv. 11 and 20
   again; in v. 20 the Greek verb may mean "have ben-
   efit" or "have joy."

The Occasion for Philemon

The short Letter to Philemon exhibits beauty, charm, and tact. It may serve also as a good example and challenge for reading with understanding. The time and place of composition of Philemon must be associated with Colossians, for Paul sent that epistle to Colossae with Tychicus, with whom Paul also sent Onesimus (Col. 4:7–9).

According to Philemon (vv. 1, 9, 10, 13, 23) Paul was in prison. The first sentence names Philemon, apparently a resident of Colossae, whom Paul calls a "fellow laborer." He was a person of some standing in the community and also hospitable, for the church met in his house (v. 2). Usually Apphia is taken to be his wife and Archippus his son. He owned a slave, Onesimus (vv. 15–16), and apparently had been converted to Christianity by Paul, for Paul reminds him, "You owe me even your own self besides" (v. 19).

Onesimus had run away from his master (vv. 15–16) and perhaps had taken some of his master's money (v. 18). After fleeing to the town (Rome or Ephesus) where Paul was in prison, Onesimus came in contact with Paul, who converted him to Christianity (v. 10)—that is, he is Paul's spiritual child, and Paul is his spiritual father. It is possible that Onesimus found a menial job in the prison where Paul was confined—perhaps bringing food to the prisoners.

We can well imagine how Paul uses every occasion and contact with others to spread the Gospel, and how Paul takes the opportunity to speak to this servant employed by the prison officials. After further conversation, Paul discovers who Onesimus really is—a runaway slave from Colossae. When Paul candidly tells him that he must make amends by returning to his master, Onesimus no doubt expresses fear that his master will treat him harshly, as was the custom in those days. On further inquiry, Paul discovers a unique coincidence—the slave's master is a person who also was converted to Christianity by Paul some years earlier (v. 19). Since Paul is about to write to the congregation at Colossae through Tychicus, he prepares a brief note to Philemon, the owner of Onesimus, and sends both epistles and Onesimus with Tychicus to Colossae (Col. 4:7–9).

STUDY QUESTION 5

Paul's approach in Philemon.

A. How does Paul use a good psychological approach? See vv. 21–22.

B. How does Paul approach a social problem of his time (slavery)?

C. Can we use a similar approach to social problems of our time?

The Content of Philemon

Paul first and foremost is asking Philemon to be lenient toward his runaway slave, who is now returning as more than a slave; he is now a fellow Christian or "beloved brother" in Christ (v. 16). Paul promises to reimburse Philemon for any financial loss caused by Onesimus (vv. 18–19). The name Onesimus means "useful" or "profitable" or "beneficial." Paul uses a play on words when he says that Onesimus, who had been "unprofitable" to Philemon, now is being "profitable" to Paul (v. 11), and when he asks Philemon for some "benefit" (v. 20; the Greek verb may mean "have benefit" or "have joy").

Paul closes his appeal with confidence that Philemon "will do even more" than Paul is requesting (v. 21). He hints that he would be glad to keep Onesimus to assist him (v. 13) but would not do so without Philemon's consent (v. 14). Frequently these statements are interpreted to mean that Paul is hinting to Philemon that he set Onesimus free. Others regard the remarks as a general compliment on Philemon's character.

While Paul uses a most tactful approach to Philemon, he also hints at a future visit to check on how Philemon actually treats Onesimus. He writes: "Prepare a guest room for me, for I trust that through your prayers I shall be granted to you" (v. 22). If Philemon does not follow Paul's advice on receiving Onesimus, Paul probably would notice some bruises on Onesimus's body.

The Value of Philemon

The Letter to Philemon is a good example of how Paul and the early church confronted social problems. Slavery was an integral part of the social structure of that day. To preach against this institution would have been considered revolutionary. Paul did not engage in any political campaign against it, but he preached a Gospel that was capable of transforming society from within. Instead of making a frontal attack on slavery—which would have invited an immediate conflict between Rome and Christianity—Paul urges a spirit of love and consideration, which would eventually result in the overthrow of the practice. Also in other epistles Paul honors the tie between slaves and masters (Col. 3:22–4:1; Eph. 6:5–9), emphasizing an approach based on the worth of the individual person, regardless of social status.

In conclusion we might mention that some scholars assume that Onesimus is the same person who later became the bishop of the church at Ephesus and was instrumental in the collection of Paul's epistles. Their reasons are twofold: (1) the name is the same, and (2) the assumption would help explain the inclusion of this brief personal note in the collection of Paul's epistles. But such an identification of the runaway slave with the bishop of Ephesus must remain merely a theory—a possibility not capable of being proved.

The Outline of Philemon

    I. Greetings (1–3)
   II. Commendation of Philemon (4–7)
  III. Plea for Onesimus (8–22)
  IV. Conclusion (23–25)

12. *Colossians and Ephesians: Letters from Prison*

STUDY QUESTION 1

Colossians and Ephesians may be studied together.
A. *See Col. 4:7–9 and Eph. 6:21–22.*
B. *See Col. 4:3, 10, 18 and Eph. 3:1; 4:1; 6:20.*
C. *See Col. 3:18–4:1 and Eph. 5:22–6:9.*

Colossians and Ephesians are usually studied together for several reasons. Paul wrote both epistles and sent them at the same time to the respective readers through the same individual, Tychicus, who was accompanied by Onesimus as he was delivering the Letter to Philemon (Col. 4:7–9; Eph. 6:21–22). Both letters were written from prison (Col. 4:3, 10, 18; Eph. 3:1; 4:1; 6:20). The contents of Colossians and Ephesians are similar and at times even overlap. Each epistle, for example, contains a "table of duties" (Col. 3:18–4:1; Eph. 5:22–6:9), and the themes of these letters are complementary—Colossians stresses "Christ, the Head of the church," while Ephesians emphasizes "The church, the body of Christ."

Colossae

Colossae was a Phrygian city, located on the Lycus River in the eastern part of the Roman province of Asia about 125 miles east of Ephesus. The city was on a major Roman road that went from Ephesus to Laodicea and then southeast to cities in Galatia that Paul visited on his first journey (Pisidian Antioch, Iconium) and to Tarsus, Paul's birthplace.

The region was very fertile, providing excellent pastures for large flocks of sheep. The chief sources of wealth included trade in wool and the textile industry. Two other cities of the region mentioned in the New Testament are Laodicea (Col. 2:1; 4:13, 16; Rev. 3:14–22) and Hierapolis (Col. 4:13). The former was an important banking center, and the latter was a health resort known for its hot mineral springs.

All three of these cities had a considerable Jewish element since the time of Antiochus the Great (223–187 B.C.), who transplanted 2,000 Jewish families from Mesopotamia and Babylon into Phrygia and Lydia. Many of these Jews no doubt found their way into the Lycus valley. Phrygia is mentioned as being represented at Jerusalem on the day of Pentecost (Acts 2:10). By the time Paul wrote to the Colossians, however, the membership included many Gentiles (Col. 1:27; 2:13).

STUDY QUESTION 2

What clues do we have that Paul did not establish the church at Colossae? See Col. 1:4; 2:1; 1:6–7; 4:12–13.

The Origin of the Church

We do not know much about the origin of the church at Colossae. Acts does not mention any visit by Paul at Colossae on his journeys. It seems that he did not organize or visit the congregation himself. He states furthermore that he only *heard* of their faith (1:4) and that the Colossians had *not seen* his face (2:1). Moreover, he clearly indicates that the Colossians had learned the Gospel from Epaphras (1:6–7), who was a native of Colossae (4:12) and had worked there as well as in Laodicea and Hierapolis (4:13).

The deduction of most scholars is that while Paul was in Ephesus on his third journey he came into contact with individuals from the Lycus valley, among whom were Epaphras and Philemon (Col. 4:12; Philemon 19, 23). These individuals then carried the Gospel to the eastern part of the province of Asia. Luke indicates as much when he writes that while Paul was at Ephesus "all who dwelt in Asia heard the word of the Lord Jesus, both Jews and Greeks"

(Acts 19:10). In some manuscripts Paul refers to Epaphras as "a faithful minister of Christ on your behalf" (Col. 1:7), for his preaching at Colossae was an extension of Paul's own ministry at Ephesus. It seems also that the house of Philemon was a center of assembly for the Colossian church (Philemon 2).

STUDY QUESTION 3

Why did Paul write Colossians?

A. *Note three elements of a new teaching to which the Colossians were exposed.*
   1. *See Col. 2:8.*
   2. *See Col. 2:11, 16.*
   3. *See Col. 2:21, 23.*
B. *What seems to be the underlying error in the new teaching? See Col. 2:8, 20 and 2:18. Does this new teaching supplement or distort the Gospel?*
C. *What does Paul emphasize in refuting the new teaching? See Col. 2:2–3; 2:9; 2:10; 1:28; 1:15–23.*

The Occasion for Colossians

While Paul was in prison (either at Rome or Ephesus), Epaphras came to him with news concerning the church at Colossae. Epaphras praised the Colossians for their faith, their love toward all the saints, and the fruit of the Gospel evident in their lives (1:3–8). But their loyalty to Christ was being undermined by a new teaching. Epaphras apparently needed advice from Paul, since it claimed to supplement, not contradict, the Gospel. He sought Paul's advice on how to deal with the new teaching, which was threatening the Gospel of God's grace.

The new teaching was similar in several respects to the Gospel preached by Epaphras and Paul. Both claimed to be a universal religion, benefiting Gentiles as well as Jews. Both taught that by nature there was a huge gulf between God and human beings. Both taught a redemption, an atonement between God and human beings. But they differed concerning the type of redemption and atonement. The Gospel preached by Paul and Epaphras taught that the only means of redemption or atonement was by God's grace through the life, death, and resurrection of Jesus Christ.

But the Gospel of Jesus' atonement seemed too simple to some at Colossae. They were adding to the Gospel of God's grace by stressing three elements: (1) a secret profound knowledge and a type of philosophy in addition to or in place of faith (2:8); (2) a stress on various rituals such as circumcision (2:11), food, drink, festivals, new moons, and sabbaths (2:16); and (3) an abstinence from certain food (2:21) and harsh treatment of the human body (2:23). These elements did not add to the Gospel of God's grace but distorted it by insisting on other requirements in addition to what Christ already had fully accomplished for the redemption and salvation of sinful human beings.

The references to "worship of angels" (2:18) and to "elemental spirits of the universe" (2:8, 20)—also translated as "basic principles of the world"—give a clue to the underlying error of the new teaching spread by some at Colossae. It was promoting other divine powers besides Christ as mediators of human redemption. The observance of rituals and the abstinence from certain foods no doubt were claimed to be the means of appeasing these divine powers. In brief, the new teaching obscured and undermined the Gospel by denying the complete sufficiency of Christ's atonement. It was so dangerous because it claimed merely to supplement the Gospel of God's grace, while in reality it was distorting or changing it. Those who proclaimed the new teaching were claiming to be elevating themselves to a certain perfection that was considered to be lacking in other Christians. There were, in their opinion, two levels of Christians—the ordinary believers through faith (considered inferior Christians) and the full and complete Christians, who were regarded as superior because of additional ritualistic and ascetic practices. The new teaching was in essence an attack on the sufficiency of Christ and His redemption by adding human achievements to the power of the cross of Christ.

Paul treats the danger of the new teaching in Col. 2. In the next chapter another occasion for writing the epistle is apparent. Some members, apparently among the Gentile converts, showed a tendency to return to pagan conduct, particularly to sexual sins and idolatry (3:5–11).

Apparently it was a coincidence that Paul was faced with the problems at Colossae at the same time that he was ready to send Onesimus back to Philemon at Colossae. So, "killing two birds with one stone," Paul sends the Epistle to the Colossians with Tychicus, who is accompanied by Onesimus, one of whom will deliver the brief Letter to Philemon.

The Content of Colossians

As noted above, the theme of Colossians is "Christ, the Head of the church." Since the new teaching at Colossae attempted to add to the Gospel of Christ as our complete Redeemer, Paul emphasizes in several places the all-sufficiency of Christ, who needs no ritualistic, ascetic, or philosophic additions to achieve salvation. Paul clearly and emphatically states that in Christ are hidden "*all the treasures of wisdom and knowledge*" (2:2–3), that in Christ *all the fullness* of the Godhead dwells (2:9), and that Christians attain *fullness* of life in Him, who is the *head* of all principality and power (2:10). Christians are "perfect" in Christ and do not need to rely on any additional practices for completeness (1:28).

It is around the sufficiency of Christ and His Gospel that Paul arranges his letter. His method of refuting error is noteworthy. Without devoting a lot of space to denouncing the false teaching, he clearly shows that the error lies in an inadequate view of the person and work of Christ. Therefore he explains the nature and mission of Jesus, His place in the universe, His relation to the church, and His complete sufficiency for all Christians.

After an introduction of greeting, thanksgiving, and prayer, which reviews the good report of Epaphras (1:1–14), Paul elaborates on Christ's person and work (1:15 23). He shows Christ in His relation to God, to creation, and to the church. Jesus is the living manifestation of God Himself. He was active in creation; He existed before created existence; He is first in power and position; He brought into being God's new creation, the church, and is its Head. Through His death and resurrection we have been redeemed. There is need for nothing else for our salvation.

The next section discusses Paul's task as an apostle (1:24 2:7). His ministry to the whole church is to make known the mystery of God, which is Christ Himself. Paul then shows his concern for the believers at Colossae and the neighboring area, particularly Laodicea. He warns them, praises them, and appeals to them to continue to live in Christ.

Then follows the section on the new teaching, which we discussed above (2:8–3:4). Paul describes it as hollow and deceptive philosophy. Elements derived from Judaism were the insistence on circumcision, the regulations about food and drink, and the observation of the Jewish festival calendar. Rooted in pagan philosophy was the tendency to worship angels and elemental spirits of the universe. This mixture of pagan philosophy and Judaic legalism was attractive but deceptive. It threatened to divide the church into those who were "spiritual" and those who were "ordinary" Christians. Paul's answer is to show that the Colossians already possessed all they needed in Christ and His Gospel of God's grace. They needed no additions to the work and person of Christ, who is all-sufficient.

In the next section (3:5–4:6) Paul treats the life of a Christian. Being in Christ means a departure from a former sinful, selfish life and the adoption of a new way of life modeled on Christ. Instead of indulging in sexual sins, greed, anger, slander, etc., the Christian practices kindness, patience, forgiveness, and love. Christian virtues are stressed particularly in the "table of duties" (3:18–4:1), which describes the relationships between wives and husbands, children and parents, servants and masters. Finally the Christian is steadfast in prayer, in thanksgiving to God, and in good conduct toward outsiders.

The conclusion presents personal items concerning Tychicus, the bearer of the epistle, Onesimus, the returning slave, and Epaphras, the pastor at Colossae (4:7–18).

Some readers today may ask why this letter was sent through Tychicus and not through Epaphras. We do not know definitely, but we may guess at the reason. Since Paul calls Epaphras his fellow prisoner (Philemon 23), it could be that Epaphras's association with Paul led to a simultaneous arrest of Epaphras. Or Epaphras may have chosen to remain with Paul for some time before returning to Colossae. Or Tychicus may have been Paul's secretary.

Outline of Colossians

 I. Introduction (1:1–14)
 II. The complete sufficiency of Christ (1:15–23)
 III. The apostleship of Paul (1:24–2:7)
 IV. The false teaching (2:8–3:4)
 V. The life in Christ (3:5–4:6)
 VI. Conclusion (4:7–18)

STUDY QUESTION 4

Many scholars believe that Ephesians was a circular letter and was not addressed only to Ephesus.

A. **What clues to this view are present in Eph. 1:15 and 3:2 when compared with Acts 20:31 (addressed to the elders from Ephesus)?**
B. **How may this theory help explain Col. 4:16?**
C. **What other circular letters are in the New Testament? See Gal. 1:2; 1 Peter 1:1; Rev. 1:4, 11.**

Letter from Laodicea

In Col. 4:16 Paul writes: "When this epistle is read among you, see that it is read also in the church of the Laodiceans, and that you likewise read the epistle from Laodicea." What should we make of the phrase "the epistle from Laodicea"?

A number of suggestions have been made—for example, that it refers to Philemon or to a letter of Paul that has been lost. Perhaps the best theory is that this term refers to the Epistle to the Ephesians.

In support of this theory we may note that Paul's statement implies that the two epistles (Colossians and "from Laodicea") apparently were companion letters and that each church (Colossae and Laodicea) would profit from reading both. As stated previously, Ephesians and Colossians are quite similar in several respects. Also, as we shall note soon, Ephesians seems to have been a circular letter, written to several congregations in the Lycus valley. Tychicus then would stop at the various churches in the Lycus valley on the way to Colossae. The town he would visit immediately before reaching Colossae would have been Laodicea (since he was coming from the west—Rome or Ephesus). Therefore Paul could refer to a circular letter that would reach Colossae just after being read at Laodicea as "the epistle from Laodicea."

Later, according to this theory, when Paul's epistles were collected, a copy of this letter was secured from Ephesus, the present title was added, and "in Ephesus" was inserted in the first verse.

Ephesians as a Circular Letter

If the theory is correct that Paul's "epistle from Laodicea" is really Ephesians, the corollary is that he originally composed Ephesians for a group of congregations in the Roman province of Asia, which included also the church at Ephesus. What are some other reasons for this deduction?

Paul says that Tychicus will deliver Ephesians at the same time he is to bring two other epistles to Colossae—Colossians and Philemon (Eph. 6:21–22; Col. 4:7–9). It seems then that the destination of Ephesians was not limited to Ephesus on the western coast but included the Lycus valley. Paul, moreover, had spent two and a half to three years in Ephesus but had not been in the Lycus valley. From Ephesians it is clear that Paul did not know the readers or addressees personally, for he says that he merely "heard" of their faith (Eph. 1:15) and that they merely "heard" of Paul's work (Eph. 3:2). It would be strange to write in that way to people with whom he had spent several years.

Furthermore there are no specific details or problems or news items linking this epistle with any particular congregation; rather, the content is very general and suitable for all the congregations. In all of Paul's other epistles to congregations the immediate occasion for writing is clear from the text; but Ephesians is an exception to this rule. It is also noteworthy that the earliest manuscripts of this letter do not contain "in Ephesus" in the first verse.

The conclusion, accepted by many scholars, is that Paul wrote Ephesians as a circular letter to churches in the Roman province of Asia, including Hierapolis, Laodicea, and Colossae in the Lycus valley. The writing of a circular epistle to several congregations is not unique, since Paul did the very same thing in the case of the various churches he organized on his first journey—the letter that we know as his Epistle to the Galatians. Incidentally, 1 Peter (1:1) and Revelation (1:4, 11) are also circular documents—so this practice was not unknown to Paul and his times.

The Occasion for Ephesians

Since Ephesians seems to be a circular document and has no specific references to particular problems, the occasion for writing Ephesians probably is to be associated with the writing of Colossians, since these two epistles contain so much common material and are delivered by the same courier, Tychicus. It has been calculated that 70 percent of Colossians overlaps Ephesians and that 50 percent of Ephesians occurs also in Colossians.

We have noted that Paul's primary occasion for writing Colossians was the threat of a new false teaching at Colossae. According to Paul's information from Epaphras, the church at Colossae was being threatened by this new teaching, but Paul realized that other congregations might also be in danger of doctrinal corruption. He no doubt thought it advisable to compose a general document for all the churches in the Lycus valley—a document containing a fuller statement about God's plan of salvation for the world through Christ and about His church. Such a full treatment of God's plan would be the best protection against the spread of the new false teaching into other cities in the Lycus valley. Christians equipped with the truths contained in Ephesians would be less likely to be swayed by the philosophic speculations that were troubling the Colossians.

Such an occasion for composing Ephesians would account for the overlapping of much material in Colossians and Ephesians. In Colossians Paul firmly refutes the errors related to him by Epaphras. In Ephesians he presents principles that he hopes will guard against the spreading of these errors. Colossians deals directly with the false teaching. Ephesians challenges the congregations to fuller understanding and maturity.

STUDY QUESTION 5

The theme of Ephesians is stated in Eph. 2:10.

A. How and in what chapters does Paul develop the first part of the verse?

B. How and in what chapters does Paul develop the second part of the verse?

C. Note how Paul frequently develops his letters with a doctrinal section followed by a practical section.

Content of Ephesians

The primary message of Ephesians is that the church is the body of Christ, while Colossians emphasizes Christ as the Head of the church. Some scholars see the theme of Ephesians summarized in Eph. 2:10: "For we are His workmanship, created in Christ Jesus for good works, which God prepared beforehand that we should walk in them." On the basis of this theme, Ephesians would consist of two large divisions. Chapters 1–3 would treat the church as God's workmanship created in Christ Jesus, while chapters 4–6 would emphasize that the church is created for good works. That is, a doctrinal section comes first, then a practical section.

Paul begins by describing God's plan of salvation as conceived from eternity. Before the creation of the world, God chose us. His plan involves the redemptive work of Christ, who is now the Head of the church, and the work of the Holy Spirit. God's plan, carried out when He raised Jesus from the dead and put Him in supreme control of the universe, is active in us also (1:3–23).

Salvation in Christ is a free gift. In our sinful nature we could never enjoy fellowship with God. But Jesus took the death we deserved on Himself. God has given us a new life through Christ—without any merit on our part—and made us to be part of a new creation with new life and spiritual power (2:1–10). His plan broke the barriers separating Jews and Gentiles. Christ's redemptive work is the only means of peace with God for all human beings regardless of race, color, sex, social status (2:11–22).

Paul serves primarily as a missionary to the Gentiles in preaching God's plan of salvation. He is instrumental in developing a new phase of God's plan—bringing people of all nations together in Christ and His church. Paul prays that the church may have understanding, love, and strength (3:1–21).

The second large division (chapters 4–6) describes the life and work of Christians. They are to demonstrate unity, since they have a common faith, loyalty, and purpose. They have one Master, Christ, who is the Head of the church, which is His body (4:1–16). Christians should manifest a new life, discarding old selfish ways. The new life involves honesty without grudging, spite, or bitterness; rather, it is influenced by a spirit of forgiveness (4:17–5:20).

The new life also permeates the Christian family and household. It affects the relationships between husband and wife, children and parents, and masters and servants. The intimate physical union between husband and wife illustrates the close spiritual union between Christ and His church (5:21–6:9). To maintain the new life in Christ and His church, spiritual weapons are needed, for a Christian with God's help must defeat powerful forces (6:10–20).

STUDY QUESTION 6

What important teaching does Paul discuss in Eph. 1:3–14?

A. How do Eph. 2:8–9 and Matt. 23:37 support the teaching?

B. What comfort does this teaching give to Christians who are concerned about their spiritual condition at the hour of death?

Ephesians 1:3–14

In Eph. 1 (and in Romans 8:29–30) Paul treats a topic that is very important but difficult to present—God's election of believers from eternity. We here present a brief diagram in order to explain the importance and the comfort of this teaching:

Source of Salvation	*Source of Damnation*	
1. man	man	(synergistic)
2. God	God	(Calvinistic)
3. God	man	(Scriptural)
(Eph. 2:8–9)	(Matt. 23:37)	

The first two sets of answers are logical deductions according to human reason. If man is the source of salvation, man must also be the source of damnation. Or if God is the source of one, He must also be the source of the other. But we do not derive our doctrine from human logic. Scripture is the only source of Christian doctrine. And Scripture teaches the third set of answers: God is the only source of salvation (Eph. 2:8–9); man is the only source of damnation (Matt. 23:37). We are saved only by God's grace, and even our faith is the work of God the Holy Spirit; rejection of God's grace is completely the fault of human beings.

The vertical line between the two columns indicates that the Gospel (salvation, left column) must be kept separate from Law (damnation, right column).

Both Law and Gospel must be preached, but they must never be mingled. The doctrine of eternal election, therefore, is most comforting. When Christians, particularly in later years of life, ponder their spiritual situation and wonder whether they will remain in faith at the hour of death, the doctrine of election offers assurance. If faith were the accomplishment of the Christian, fear that faith might fail before death would present some cause for alarm. But thanks to our election to salvation from eternity by God's grace, our faith is the result of His choice and is sustained by His Holy Spirit through Word and Sacrament. Therefore Christians can be assured with Paul: "Who shall separate us from the love of Christ? . . . . For I am persuaded that neither death nor life, nor angels nor principalities nor powers, nor things present nor things to come, nor height nor depth, nor any other created thing, shall be able to separate us from the love of God which is in Christ Jesus our Lord'' (Rom. 8:35, 38–39).

Outline of Ephesians

I. Introduction (1:1–2)
II. Doctrinal: The church is God's workmanship created in Christ Jesus (1:3–3:21)
    A. God's plan from eternity (1:3–23)
    B. Free salvation in Christ for all nations (2:1–22)
    C. Paul's mission to the Gentiles (3:1–21)
III. Practical: The church is created for good works (4:1–6:20)
    A. Unity through diverse gifts (4:1–16)
    B. New life in Christ (4:17–5:20)
    C. Christian family and household (5:21–6:9)
    D. Spiritual warfare (6:10–20)
IV. Conclusion (6:21–24)

13. *1 Timothy, Titus, 2 Timothy: Pastoral Letters*

*T*he term "pastoral" comes from the Latin word *pastor*, which means "shepherd." The phrase "Pastoral Letters" means that these three epistles were written to Timothy and Titus, who were acting as Paul's representatives in shepherding Christian congregations in Paul's absence.

The term "pastoral" was first applied to 1 Timothy by Thomas Aquinas in the 13th century. Later 2 Timothy and Titus were also included under this title, although 2 Timothy is rather a personal letter, while 1 Timothy and Titus are addressed also to congregations.

These three epistles do not fit into the scheme of Paul's journeys as recorded in Acts. Therefore he must have written them after he was released from his first Roman imprisonment. Church tradition relates that Paul did carry out his previous plans of spreading the Gospel into Spain. Whether the trip to Spain occurred before, after, or in between the writing of these epistles is not certain. We must admit, therefore, that various orders of events are possible in tracing Paul's activities after his first Roman imprisonment. The next section provides only a *probable* sequence of events.

STUDY QUESTION 1

Acts closes with Paul's first Roman imprisonment (Acts 28:30).

A. *Construct a probable order of his later travels on the basis of the following passages: Rom. 15:28; Titus 1:5; 1 Tim. 1:3; Titus 3:12; 2 Tim. 4:20; 4:13.*
B. *Why would Paul have left his cloak, books, and parchments at Troas?*

Probable Order of Events

1. After two years of "house arrest" at Rome (Acts 28:30) Paul was released.

2. Paul's trip to Spain may have taken place immediately after his release. His previous plan was to go from Rome to Spain (Rom. 15:28). Church history records that Paul made the trip; no one in antiquity seems to have questioned its occurrence.

3. Paul probably returned to the eastern Mediterranean by way of the island of Crete, where he left Titus in charge (Titus 1:5).

4. Paul then probably stopped at Ephesus, where he left Timothy in charge (1 Tim. 1:3).

5. Paul then could have proceeded to Macedonia, where he wrote 1 Timothy (1 Tim. 1:3).

6. Either at Macedonia or during a journey to Nicopolis in Epirus Paul wrote the Epistle to Titus. He planned to spend the winter at Nicopolis, where Titus was to join him after being relieved in Crete by Artemas and Tychicus (Titus 3:12).

7. Paul says that he visited Troas, Corinth, and Miletus (2 Tim. 4:13, 20). It is likely that he went from Corinth to Miletus and on to Troas, where he was arrested and sent to Rome. This order would explain why he left his cloak, books, and parchments at Troas—because he was arrested there suddenly.

8. From Rome during his second imprisonment Paul wrote 2 Timothy.

9. According to church tradition Paul was martyred at Rome during the reign of Nero.

STUDY QUESTION 2

What does the New Testament tell us about Timothy and his relation to Paul? See Acts 16:1–3; 2 Tim. 1:5; 3:15; 1 Cor. 4:17 (and 1 Tim. 1:2 and 2 Tim. 1:2);

1 Tim. 4:14 (and 2 Tim. 1:6); 1 Tim. 1:3; 1 Thess. 3:1–2; 1 Cor. 16:10; Phil. 2:19–23; 1 Tim. 5:23.

Timothy

Since Paul used Timothy and Titus so frequently as his representatives, it should be in place to summarize the information that the New Testament gives about them.

Timothy, a resident of Lystra in Galatia, was the son of a Greek father and a Jewish mother, Eunice (Acts 16:1–3; 2 Tim. 1:5). In his youth he had received instruction in the Old Testament from his mother and his grandmother, Lois (2 Tim. 1:5; 3:15). It is interesting to note that he was a son of a mixed marriage and had not been circumcised as a child (Acts 16:3). His conversion to Christianity no doubt occurred when Paul was at Lystra on his first journey (Acts 14:8–20), since Paul refers to him as his child in the Lord and his child in faith (1 Cor. 4:17; 1 Tim. 1:2; cf. 2 Tim. 1:2). Paul no doubt also converted Timothy's mother on his first visit to Lystra, since on his second visit she is referred to as a Jewish woman who was a believer (Acts 16:1).

On his visit to Lystra at the beginning of his second journey, Paul decided to take Timothy along as an assistant, had him circumcised as a concession to Jewish prejudice (Acts 16:3), and had him ordained to the ministry by the elders, with Paul also participating (1 Tim. 4:14; 2 Tim. 1:6).

From the Pastoral Letters we see that Paul used Timothy as his representative at Ephesus (1 Tim. 1:3). Previously Paul used Timothy as his representative to Thessalonica (1 Thess. 3:1–2), to Corinth (1 Cor. 4:17; 16:10), and to Philippi (Phil. 2:19–23). Timothy was faithful and loyal, though apparently somewhat timid and lacking in robust health (1 Cor. 16:10–11; 1 Tim. 5:23).

STUDY QUESTION 3

What does the New Testament tell us about Titus and his relation to Paul? See Titus 1:4; Gal. 2:1–5; 2 Cor. 2:13; 7:6–7; 8:6; 8:23; 12:18; Titus 1:5; 3:12; 2 Tim. 4:10.

Titus

For some unknown reason the name of Titus does not occur in Acts, but does come up in Paul's epistles. Some scholars have conjectured that Titus may have been the brother of Luke, the author of Acts, who purposely does not mention the name of his brother. Both Titus and Luke were of Greek descent.

Titus probably was converted by Paul directly from paganism, for Paul refers to him as his true child in a common faith (Titus 1:4). His home probably was in Syrian Antioch, where Paul and Barnabas preached for a year before the first journey (Acts 11:26) and where Titus perhaps became one of their converts. When Paul went to Jerusalem the second time, he took Titus along and later wrote of him as an example of a Gentile who was not compelled to be circumcised (Gal. 2:1–5).

It is on Paul's third journey that we next hear of Titus, who apparently remained at Syrian Antioch after his trip to Jerusalem. We may suppose that Titus accompanied Paul on the third journey, for at Ephesus Titus is one of Paul's assistants. At least Paul sent Titus to Corinth (2 Cor. 2:13; 7:6–7; 8:6; 12:18), no doubt from Ephesus, for Titus reported to Paul in Macedonia on the conditions at Corinth.

We hear no more of Titus until he is mentioned in the Pastoral Letters. Paul and Titus had been engaged in missionary work in Crete, where Paul left him as his representative (Titus 1:5). Paul asked Titus to join him at Nicopolis (Titus 3:12). Later Titus was with Paul in Rome during Paul's second Roman imprisonment. At that time he may also have gone to Dalmatia temporarily, no doubt on an errand for Paul (2 Tim. 4:10).

Paul had a high regard for Titus or he would not have relied on him as his assistant to deal with the serious troubles at Corinth. Paul's respect for Titus is apparent from his references to Titus as his child in the common faith (Titus 1:4), as his brother (2 Cor. 2:13), and as his partner and fellow worker (2 Cor. 8:23).

The Occasion for 1 Timothy

There are two main reasons why Paul wrote the First Letter to Timothy, who then was stationed at Ephesus. The congregation there needed guidance on church administration as well as a warning against a false teaching that was endangering the church. Some years previous, on the return trip of his third journey, Paul had predicted to the Ephesian elders that false teaching would creep into their congregation (Acts 20:29–30). And so it did. Apparently Paul had to deal with some troublemakers before he left Timothy in charge (1 Tim. 1:19–20). Since Paul's return to Ephesus was being delayed, he gave his advice to Timothy and the congregation in this epistle. At that time Timothy was acting as Paul's representative at Ephesus, as he had at Corinth, Thessalonica, and Philippi (1 Cor. 4:17; 1 Thess. 3:1–2; Phil. 2:19–23).

The false teaching current at Ephesus was not unlike that which Paul had found at Colossae. There was an emphasis on knowledge (*gnosis* in Greek; hence the movement is called Gnosticism). This error developed more fully in the second century, but its beginnings are evident already during the life of Paul.

Its basic premise was that there is a dualism in the universe—material or physical things, which are evil in themselves, and spiritual or nonmaterial elements, which are good in themselves. According to this premise, the physical world is essentially evil since it is made up of material things. It cannot be God's creation, for matter is alien to God. Therefore human beings must be redeemed from the world of matter by a type of knowledge that comes through special revelation to a select group of individuals. Those who have this special knowledge and revelation are to free themselves from the influence of matter by abstaining from marriage and from certain foods. Sometimes, however, the negative attitude toward material things had the opposite effect; indifference to physical elements led to freedom to engage in sexual sins, which were regarded as morally indifferent.

This false teaching resulted in a denial of sin as the cause of our separation from God and in a rejection of Christ's atonement as our redemption. God is no longer the Creator of a good universe. The Old Testament is interpreted through myths and endless genealogies. The incarnation of God's Son disappears, for the divine cannot be joined with the physical. The false teaching of Gnosticism, in brief, is a denial of God's grace through faith because of Christ's redemption.

STUDY QUESTION 4

What general topics does Paul discuss in 1 Timothy?

A. What is the general topic in chapters 2 and 3?

B. What are the subdivisions in these chapters?

C. What is the general topic in chapter 4? How does this problem compare with the one in Colossians?

D. How is Timothy to deal with various members? See 1 Tim. 5:1–6:2?

Content of 1 Timothy

Paul immediately takes up the matter of false teaching in the first chapter. He charges Timothy to preserve the purity of the Gospel, reminds him of the purpose of the Law, and expresses thanks that he (Paul) has been called into God's service (1:3–20).

The next two chapters give instruction concerning church administration. Paul offers suggestions for the regulation of public worship, including the role of women in it (2:1–15). He then lays down qualifications for bishops (3:1–7) and deacons (3:8–13) and adds a personal word to Timothy (3:14–16).

Paul returns to the topic of the false teachers in chapter 4. He then discusses the proper attitude toward various groups of members—the elderly and the young (5:1–2), widows (5:3–16), the elders (5:17–25), and slaves (6:1–2). Once more Paul returns to the topic of false teachers, warning particularly against those who attempt to make a profit from religion (6:3–21).

Outline of 1 Timothy

    I. Introduction and false teaching (1:1–20)

   II. Public worship (2:1–15)

  III. Qualifications of bishops and deacons (3:1–16)

  IV. False teachers (4:1–16)

   V. Attitude toward various groups (5:1–6:2)

 VI. Concluding warning against false teachers and exhortations to Timothy (6:3–21)

The Occasion for Titus

Paul's Epistle to Titus is similar in occasion and content to 1 Timothy. Paul had worked with Titus in Crete, as he had with

Timothy at Ephesus. When Paul departed from Crete, he left Titus in charge as his representative, as he did Timothy at Ephesus. In each situation the Christians were being troubled by a false teaching of the Gnostic type, but in Crete the teaching was more Judaic than at Ephesus (Titus 1:14; 3:9).

The situation facing Titus at Crete was perhaps more complicated because the church there had been founded more recently than the church at Ephesus, and as a result it lacked solid organization. The environment at Crete also was one of low morals, and people were given especially to falsehood (Titus 1:12–13). Although we read of Cretans being present at Pentecost (Acts 2:11), it seems that the message of Peter at that time fell on deaf ears and that the church was not founded at Crete until Paul and Titus preached there after Paul's release from his first Roman imprisonment.

The immediate occasion for writing this letter perhaps was the visit of Zenas and Apollos to Crete (Titus 3:13). Paul realized that Titus and the church in Crete needed encouragement. That Titus's position was only temporary is seen from the fact that Paul intended to send another worker to replace him so that he then could rejoin Paul at Nicopolis (Titus 3:12).

Paul's purpose in writing to Titus, as in his first letter to Timothy, was primarily twofold—to give guidance on church administration and to warn against a false teaching that was troubling the church.

While the occasion and content of Titus and 1 Timothy are similar, each describing the qualifications of bishops, there is one significant difference. Among the requirements for a bishop at Ephesus Paul specifically states that he must not be a "novice," which means "a recent convert" (1 Tim. 3:6). Paul omits this demand, however, in writing to Titus (Titus 1:7–9). The reason is clear. Since the church at Ephesus had existed for five to eight years, Paul could include the qualification of experience for a bishop of the church at Ephesus. Its omission from the Epistle to Titus is a further indication that Christianity had taken hold at Crete only recently and that almost all the Christians there were recent converts.

In brief, while both Timothy and Titus were to deal with similar false teachings, Titus was to *establish* order in a church founded only recently, while Timothy was to *restore* order in a Christian community that had existed for some time.

STUDY QUESTION 5

The content of Paul's Letter to Titus.

A. *How does the first chapter of Titus compare with the third chapter of 1 Timothy? What two words are interchangeable in Titus 1:5, 7?*

B. *How does the second chapter of Titus compare with 1 Tim. 5:1–6:2?*

C. *Why do you suppose Paul emphasizes Christian conduct in Titus 3:1–8? Note Titus 1:10–16.*

Content of Titus

Paul's Epistle to Titus treats three main topics, which in general correspond to its division into three chapters. The first chapter presents the requirements for the elders or bishops, who are to oppose the current false teaching. It is pertinent to note that in this section the two terms, elder and bishop, seem to be used interchangeably (Titus 1:5, 7). That is, the church administration had not developed into the organization of the second century, when there was a decided difference in the function of these two offices. The interchangeable use of the two terms, elder and bishop, is a good argument for the genuineness of these Pastoral Letters—that they were written by Paul and not by a second-century forger.

Chapter 2 develops specific moral instructions for different groups in the church—older men (2:1–2), older women (2:3–5), younger men (2:6–8), slaves (2:9–10)—and concludes with a summary of Christian moral life in general (2:11–15). The third chapter expands on Christian morality, teaching the avoidance of hatred and argument and demanding meekness, kindness, and obedience (3:1–8). The letter concludes with advice to Titus and some personal items (3:9–15).

While the content of Titus and 1 Timothy is similar in many respects, it is pertinent to notice a difference in emphasis. In 1 Timothy there is more stress on false teaching and false teachers. In Titus the emphasis is more on Christian conduct. No doubt conditions in Crete led Paul to place more stress on conduct in writing to Titus than in writing to Timothy at Ephesus. The recent conversion of the Christians at Crete, living in a morally corrupt environment, caused Paul to emphasize Christian conduct.

Outline of Titus

I. Introduction (1:1–4)
II. Requirements for elders/bishops in the face of false teaching (1:5–16)
III. Moral instruction for various groups (2:1–15)
IV. Christian morality in general (3:1–8)
V. Advice to Titus (3:9–11)
VI. Conclusion (3:12–15)

STUDY QUESTION 6

Paul's final letter: 2 Timothy.

A. **What is Paul's situation when he writes 2 Timothy? See 2 Tim. 1:8, 16; 2:9; 4:6–8, 11, 16, 17.**
B. **What clues indicate that Timothy is at Ephesus? See 2 Tim. 4:19 and 1:16–18; 2 Tim. 2:17 and 1 Tim. 1:19–20; 1 Tim. 1:3.**
C. **What three topics does Paul stress in 2 Timothy? See 2 Tim. 1:13–14; 2:3–13; 2:14–19 (and 4:1–8).**

The Occasion for 2 Timothy

When Paul wrote 2 Timothy, he was again a prisoner in Rome (2 Tim. 1:8, 16), but the circumstances were different. During the first imprisonment Paul was allowed to live in his own rented dwelling (or at his own expense) and was accessible to everyone who wished to see him (Acts 28:30–31). Now Paul is in chains like a criminal (2 Tim. 1:16; 2:9), hard to find (1:17), almost alone (4:11), and expecting death (4:6–8). At a preliminary hearing, the testimony of a pagan metalworker had proved damaging and no one supported Paul (4:14–16). Since Paul's status as a Roman citizen had been recognized, he would not have to face the lions in the arena (4:17).

As he awaits eventual execution, Paul writes his last will and testament to Timothy, eager to see him once more before Paul meets his Lord. He wants Timothy to come to Rome from Ephesus before the winter storms make travel by sea too dangerous (1:4; 4:9, 21). Timothy is to bring Mark along (4:11), as well as Paul's cloak, books, and parchments left at Troas (4:13). The parchments

159

may have included copies of Paul's correspondence (for it was customary for a person to keep copies of his letters). The books may have included portions of the Old Testament.

Although Paul does not state in so many words that Timothy was at Ephesus, several indications point to this conclusion. Paul asks Timothy to greet the household of Onesiphorus (4:19), who was a resident at Ephesus (1:16–18). He refers to a false teacher by the name of Hymenaeus (2:17), who no doubt is the same person mentioned in 1 Tim. 1:19–20. The request to bring the cloak, books, and parchments left at Troas implies that Timothy was at a place from which his trip to Rome could lead through Troas. Finally, in 1 Timothy we are told that Timothy was at Ephesus (1 Tim. 1:3).

Content of 2 Timothy

Paul's final epistle has a threefold emphasis. Timothy is: (1) to preserve the Gospel in its purity, (2) to be ready to suffer, and (3) to guard against false teachers. Paul is encouraging Timothy to continue to be strong in his ministry as a good soldier of Christ Jesus (2 Tim. 2:3). Three times he speaks of suffering hardships (1:8; 2:3; 4:5). Timothy must have boldness in preaching the Gospel in its fullness (4:1–2). He must be firm in the face of the false teachers who appeal to the itching ears of the people (4:3–5).

The letter is a plea from a veteran missionary to a younger associate. Timothy is to rekindle the gift of God within him (1:3–7), is not to be ashamed of his witness (1:8–18), and is to accept his share of suffering (2:1–13). In dealing with false teachers Timothy must handle the Word rightly (2:14–19), keep himself pure (2:20–26), and follow the example of Paul (3:1–17), who is at the end of his career (4:1–8).

Outline of 2 Timothy

    I. Introduction (1:1–5)
   II. Appeal to remain loyal and guard the truth (1:6–18)
  III. Encouragement to face hardships (2:1–13)
  IV. Charge to combat false teachers (2:14–26)
   V. Dangers of the last days (3:1–17)
  VI. Correction of error (4:1–8)

The Value of the Pastoral Epistles

Although missionaries and parish pastors have found these letters to be extremely helpful in their ministries, the Pastoral Epistles should not be neglected by the laity. They show the dangers of false teaching in the church and abound in clear statements of some of the great truths of Christianity. Several examples should be sufficient: Jesus came to save sinners (1 Tim. 1:12–17); the grace of God has come for all people (Titus 2:11–14); Christians are assured of living and reigning with Jesus in eternity (2 Tim. 2:11–13); all Scripture is inspired and profitable (2 Tim. 3:16–17).

14. James and Hebrews: God's Grace and Judaism

STUDY QUESTION 1

What does the New Testament tell us about James the brother of Jesus? See Matt. 13:55; Mark 6:3; John 7:5; 1 Cor. 15:7; 9:3–6; Acts 12:17; Gal. 1:19; 2:9; 2:11–12; Acts 15:13–21; 21:17–18.

Author of James

The author identifies himself as "James, a servant of God and of the Lord Jesus Christ" (1:1). Since James, the son of Zebedee and brother of John, was beheaded by Herod Agrippa I in A.D. 44 (Acts 12:1–2), the most likely candidate for authorship is James the brother of Jesus. ("Brother" may indicate a son of Mary and Joseph or a half brother, a son of Joseph by a previous marriage. Either interpretation is possible, since Scripture does not teach the perpetual virginity of Mary.)

Apparently James did not accept Jesus as the promised Messiah during Jesus' ministry on earth, for we read: "Even His brothers did not believe in Him" (John 7:5). The names of Jesus' brothers are recorded twice in the New Testament: James, Joses (or Joseph), Simon, and Judas (Matt. 13:55; Mark 6:3). It seems that James accepted Jesus as the Messiah after the resurrected Christ appeared to him (1 Cor. 15:7). James and the other brothers then did undertake some missionary journeys, perhaps in Palestine (1 Cor. 9:3–6), but James seems to have concentrated his work in Jerusalem.

After the death of James the brother of John in A.D. 44, James the brother of Jesus becomes the recognized leader of the Christian church at Jerusalem. When Peter miraculously escapes from prison in A.D. 44, he asks that his escape be reported "to James and to the brethren" (Acts 12:17). In writing to the Galatians, Paul ranks James as an apostle (Gal. 1:19) and mentions him ahead of Peter and John as "pillars" of the church at Jerusalem (Gal. 2:9). Paul refers to people who came to Antioch from Jerusalem as those who "came from James" (Gal. 2:11–12). At the Apostolic Council at Jerusalem the voice of James is most prominent (Acts 15:13–21) and no doubt he is the main writer of the circular letter issued by the Council (Acts 15:23–29). When Paul returns to Jerusalem after his third journey, he reports "to James" (Acts 21:17–18).

A comparison of the Epistle of James with the speech and letter attributed to James at the Apostolic Council reveals a number of similarities. Both have the same form of greeting—*chairein* in Greek (Acts 15:23; James 1:1), a form of greeting found only one other time in the New Testament (Acts 23:26). Both contain a similar exhortation for "brothers" to "listen" (Acts 15:13; James 2:5). Both contain an unusual word for "visit" (Acts 15:14; James 1:27). These and other parallels are remarkable because they occur in a brief letter and in the short passage attributed to James at the Apostolic Council. Such similarities do not *prove* that James is the author of this epistle, but they support the other arguments in favor of the traditional authorship.

According to early church history James was a model of Jewish piety. One source says that he spent so much time on his knees in prayer that they became as hard as the knees of a camel. Even the nonbelieving Jews respected James, for he was called "James the Just." He died a martyr's death (A.D. 62 or 66), and some pious Jews later regarded the fall of Jerusalem in A.D. 70 as divine punishment for his martyrdom.

The question may arise as to why James was elevated over Peter as leader of the church at Jerusalem. We do not know; we may only speculate. One suggestion is that the Jewish Christians at Jerusalem never forgot that the great influx of Gentiles into the church was the outcome of the action of Peter, who went against Judaic custom by entering the house of a Gentile, Cornelius (Acts 10). The Christians at Jerusalem immediately demanded an explanation for that action (Acts 11).

STUDY QUESTION 2

What do the following passages tell us about the addressees of James: James 1:1 (twelve tribes) and 2:2 ("assembly" is "synagogue" in the Greek text); 1:2, 6; 2:6–7; 3:1–12; 4:4; 5:4? Note what Jesus said in Matt. 23:3.

The Addressees of James

The first verse states that James is writing "to the twelve tribes which are scattered abroad" (1:1). The phrase "twelve tribes" indicates that the intended readers are Jews, who in the Old Testament trace their ancestry to the 12 tribes of Israel. It is also clear from the epistle itself that James is addressing Jewish Christians. He repeatedly calls the intended readers "brothers" (or "brethren") who have been born again by the Word of God (1:18–19), who "hold the faith of our Lord Jesus Christ" (2:1), and who look for "the coming of the Lord" (5:7). Only in James—never in all the other documents of the New Testament—is the meeting place of the readers called a synagogue in the Greek text (translated "assembly" in 2:2), a term used in Jewish Christianity but not frequently elsewhere.

The general coloring of the epistle fits the Christian church in Jerusalem and in Palestine—a poor, tired, oppressed, and persecuted church—a picture that agrees with Acts and Paul's epistles, which report that Paul twice brings financial assistance to the Jewish Christians (Acts 11:27–30; Rom. 15:25–28; 1 Cor. 16:1–4; Acts 21:15–18). The evils described in the epistle, furthermore, are the besetting sins of Judaism; especially prominent is the failure to practice what is preached, as Jesus himself noted (Matt. 23:3), while sexual sins, common among Gentiles, are mentioned only once (4:4).

Since the first verse speaks of the 12 tribes "which are scattered abroad," James no doubt is addressing Jewish Christians also beyond the confines of Jerusalem and Palestine. He probably is writing also to Jewish Christians located in Samaria, Galilee, Syria, and Cilicia. The fact that he writes in Greek may indicate that the readers include the Greek-speaking Jewish Christians, known as Hellenists (Acts 6:1), who perhaps congregated in those areas.

Pertinent also to the conclusion that James is writing to Jewish Christians is the surprising number of similarities between James's epistle and the Lord's Sermon on the Mount. Both contain the following:

James	Theme	Matthew
1:2	Joy in the midst of trials	5:10–12
1:4	Exhortation to perfection	5:48
1:5	Asking for good gifts	7:7–12
1:20	Against anger	5:22
1:22	Hearers and doers of the Word	7:24–27
2:10	The whole Law to be kept	5:19
2:13	Blessings of mercy	5:7
3:18	Blessings of peacemakers	5:9
4:4	Friendship with world	6:24
4:10	Blessings of humility	5:5
4:11–12	Against judging others	7:1–5
5:2–3	Moth and rust spoiling riches	6:19
5:10	Example of prophets	5:12
5:12	Against oaths	5:33–37

We should note that although the ideas are common to both documents, James is not citing the exact words found in Matthew but is stressing the oral teaching of Jesus, which many of the Jewish Christian readers had heard from the Master.

Time and Place of James

If James the brother of the Lord is the author, the place of writing would be Jerusalem, where he was the leader of the church. Several allusions to physical conditions in Palestine confirm this deduction—references to the "early and latter rain" (James 5:7), the effect of hot winds on vegetation (1:11), the existence of salty and bitter springs (3:11–12), the cultivation of figs and olives (3:12), and the suggestions that the sea is nearby (1:6; 3:4).

The date of composition, however, is not so easy to determine. Since there is no reference to the Gentile-Jewish controversy, settled in A.D. 49 at the Apostolic Council, scholars are divided. Some date James before the controversy arose, which would be about A.D. 45, while others prefer some time after the controversy subsided, which would be shortly before the death of James in the early sixties. If James is dated around A.D. 45, it would be the earliest of all the New Testament documents.

Those who prefer the earlier date point to the apparently elementary organization in the church. That is, James mentions only the "elders of the church" (5:14) and omits any reference to bishops or deacons—thus patterning the Christian congregation largely after the Jewish synagogue. The warning against many becoming teachers (3:1) also may point to an early type of organization.

The Occasion for James

The occasion for this epistle is clearly discernible from its contents. It is not a treatise on Christian doctrine but a plea for practical Christian life. It has been compared with the wisdom literature of the Old Testament, such as Proverbs. In its 108 verses there are 54 imperatives. It draws its imagery largely from the outdoors, as Jesus did. The Epistle of James has also been called the Amos of the New Testament, since it offers stinging rebuke to social injustice.

The people were beset by many trials (1:2) and were not taking sufficient advantage of prayer (1:5). As members of the poorer class, they were suffering social injustice. Members of the laboring class (1:9), employed by the wealthier landowners, were being dragged into court (2:6–7) or were having wages withheld (5:4). Instead of showing patience and humility, the people were engaging in complaints against one another (4:11–12) and in quarrels and dissensions (4:1–3). Their attitude was materialistic and worldly (4:13–17).

In view of these conditions, which indicate that faith is not vitally operative in the lives of the people, James presents a plea for putting into practice what is preached. It is really a sermon rather than a letter. (While James has the customary introduction of a letter, the usual conclusion is absent.) It is hortatory in content, urging the Christians to live their belief in spite of their trials.

Content of James

Although James writes in clear, simple Greek instead of using the more involved sentence structure found frequently in Paul's epistles, the organization of James's content is not so simple. Some students see in James primarily parallel thoughts placed side by side without coordination or subordination. Other students, however, see a plan of organization. We shall present several attempts at structuring the content of James.

Some view the first chapter as a staccato enumeration of almost all the topics dealt with more fully later in the epistle. The proposed scheme is as follows:

Testing (1:2; 1:12–15)

Endurance (1:3; 5:7–11)
Wisdom (1:5; 3:13–18)
Prayer (1:5–8; 4:2–3; 5:13–18)
Faith (1:6; 2:14–26)
Riches (1:9–11; 2:1–13; 5:1–6)
Tongue (1:19, 26; 3:1–12)
Christianity in action (1:22–25; 2:14–26)

This scheme is reminiscent of Proverbs in the Old Testament and of the Sermon on the Mount in the New Testament (Matt. 5–7).

According to another scheme, the epistle is organized on the basis of the central theme of the blessedness of enduring trials (1:12). After a brief salutation (1:1), the topic of tests of faith is discussed in verses 2–18. Then James sets forth a series of six criteria by which the readers may test their faith:

1. Faith is tested by its attitude toward the Word of God (1:19–27).
2. Faith is tested by its reaction to social distinctions (2:1–13).
3. Faith is tested by its production of good works (2:14–26).
4. Faith is tested by its exercise of self-control (3:1–18).
5. Faith is tested by its reaction to the world (4:1–5:12).
6. Faith is tested by its reliance on prayer (5:13–18).

James then concludes with an appeal to restore those who have strayed (5:19–20).

Still another scheme views James as a series of four meditations, each expanding on one or more of the sayings of Jesus. The meditations cover the following four topics:

1. Temptation (1:2–18)
2. Law of love (1:19–2:26)
3. Evil speaking (3:1–4:12)
4. Endurance (4:13–5:20)

The saying or sayings of Jesus parallel to each of these meditations respectively would be:

1. "Do not lead us into temptation" (Matt. 6:13; Luke 11:4).
2. "You shall love the Lord your God" and "You shall love your neighbor as yourself" (Matt. 22:37, 39).
3. "Not what goes into the mouth defiles a man; but what comes out of the mouth, this defiles a man" (Matt. 15:11).
4. "He who endures to the end shall be saved" (Mark 13:13).

These are examples of attempts to organize the content of James. Another is given under the next section.

Outline of James

I. Introduction (1:1)

II. Turn to your God, the good Giver of perfect gifts (1:2–27).
   A. Turn to the God who perfects you by trial (1:2–18).
   B. Turn to the God who has implanted His Word of truth among you (1:19–27).

III. Turn to true and active faith (2:1–26).
   A. Turn from partiality toward the rich (2:1–13).
   B. Turn from mere profession to an active faith (2:14–26).

IV. Turn, teachers, to God-given wisdom (3:1–18).
   A. Turn from your sinful selves to God (3:1–12).
   B. Turn from earthly wisdom to God (3:13–18).

V. Turn to God, the Giver of the Spirit and of all grace (4:1–12).
   A. Turn to God from conformity to the world (4:1–10).
   B. Turn from the world's evil speaking (4:11–12).

VI. Turn from the world's self-assurance (4:13–5:6).
   A. Turn from worldly self-assured planning (4:13–17).
   B. Turn from worldly accumulation of wealth (5:1–6).

VII. Turn to the returning Lord (5:7–20).
   A. Rest in the Lord and wait patiently for Him (5:7–12).
   B. Let your whole life be attuned to His coming (5:13–20).

STUDY QUESTION 3

Does James 2:18–26 contradict what Paul says about faith and works? Note 2:19 for the sense in which James uses "faith." What is the relationship of good works to faith?

Luther's View of James

Perhaps a word should be said about Luther's comment that James is "an epistle of straw." No doubt Luther criticized James because the Roman Catholic Church was citing it to defend its doctrine of justification by works (2:14–26) and its "sacrament" of extreme unction (5:13–15). But there is no basic disagreement between James and Paul, for they are using "faith" in two different senses. By "faith" Paul denotes the conviction of the heart, which always brings forth good works as fruits of faith. James, however, is using faith as consisting merely of head knowledge, for he says that "even the demons believe—and tremble!" (2:19). So James insists that such a "faith" (head knowledge) without works is dead (2:26). Furthermore when he speaks of anointing with oil, he is referring to a medical practice of the day and is not giving directions for another "sacrament."

We may note, furthermore, that in calling James "an epistle of straw" Luther was not questioning the inspiration of Scripture but was rather doubting whether the Epistle of James should be included in the canon. That is, Luther was raising a historical, not a doctrinal, issue. Therefore one cannot appeal to Luther's statement as proof that he failed to view all of Scripture as God's inspired and authoritative Word (cf. 2 Tim. 3:16).

STUDY QUESTION 4

What clues indicate that Hebrews is modeled on a sermon (homily)? See Hebrews 1:1–4; 13:22–25; 2:1, 5; 5:11; 6:9; 8:1; 9:5; 11:32.

Hebrews

We called James a sermon rather than a letter. Favoring a similar view of Hebrews is the fact that it lacks an epistolary introduction (as James lacks an epistolary conclusion)—that is, the author does not identify himself or the addressees, and there is no greeting or statement of thanksgiving. Instead, Hebrews begins with a majestic sentence on the supremacy of the Son through whom God has spoken His final Word (1:1–4). In other words, it begins like a sermon.

At the end of the document the author furthermore calls what he has written a "word of exhortation" (13:22). This phrase seems to have been the normal term for the sermon that followed the reading of the Law and the Prophets in the synagogue, as was the case when Paul and Barnabas spoke in the synagogue at Antioch of Pisidia: "After the reading of the Law and the Prophets, the rulers of the synagogue sent to them, saying, 'Men and brethren, if you have any word of exhortation for the people, say on'" (Acts 13:15). Paul's "word of exhortation" at that occasion contains encouragement and warning (Acts 13:16–41)—the same characteristics found in Hebrews.

An equally pertinent clue to the sermonic character of Hebrews is the emphasis on speaking and hearing:

> Therefore we must give the more earnest heed to the things we have *heard*. (Heb. 2:1)

> He has not put the world to come, of which we *speak*, in subjection to angels. (2:5)

> . . . of whom we have much to *say*, and hard to explain, since you have become dull of *hearing*. (5:11)

> . . . though we *speak* in this manner. (6:9)

> This is the main point of what we are *saying*. (8:1)

> Of these things we cannot now *speak* in detail. (9:5)

> What more shall I *say?* For the time would fail me to *tell* . . . (11:32) (emphases added)

The general impression is that the author wishes the addressees to think of him as delivering a sermon or homily in their presence.

Open Questions

Almost all historical data concerning Hebrews are debated by students of the New Testament. In the first place, it is noted that the author does not identify himself. The early church and modern scholars, therefore, have come up with a host of suggested authors: Paul, Barnabas, Luke, Clement of Rome, Silvanus (Silas), Apollos, Philip, and Priscilla, to mention the leading candidates.

The addressees and the destination of Hebrews are also debatable topics. Some prefer a Jewish Christian group, while others favor Gentile Christian readers. Suggested destinations include Palestine, Rome, Alexandria, Colossae, Ephesus, Galatia, Asia, Syria, Antioch, Corinth, Cyprus, and Berea.

The purpose or occasion for writing varies in the opinion of many scholars. Some say it was written to warn Christians against apostasy (defection) to Judaism. Others see in Hebrews a challenge to Jewish Christians to foster world missions. Still others view it as a declaration to Gentile Christians of the absolute validity of Christianity. There are also those who regard Hebrews as counteracting some type of heresy like Jewish Gnosticism or the heresy found at Colossae.

Instead of analyzing the arguments for each suggestion, we would do better to cite some pertinent passages from Hebrews and on their basis to present some probable answers to these questions—always remembering that our suggestions are just that: probable answers to open questions.

STUDY QUESTION 5

What do the following passages tell us about the addressees of Hebrews: 13:19, 23; 5:12; 6:10; 10:32–34; 13:7; 12:4; 5:11–14; 10:25; 3:12; 6:4–8?

Pertinent Passages

That Hebrews was addressed to a specific group of Christians is clear from the fact that the author hopes to visit them soon (13:19, 23). The addressees had been Christians for some time already (5:12) and were fruitful in ministering to fellow believers (6:10). Previously they had "endured a great struggle with sufferings," had assisted those who were imprisoned, and had experienced plundering of their property (10:32–34). Apparently their former teachers had died (13:7) and now they should obey their present leaders (13:17). Their persecution had not yet resulted in the shedding of blood (12:4), which suggests that martyrdom may become a reality in the near future.

At the time of the writing of Hebrews the addressees had ceased growing in faith (5:11–14) and were neglecting the public gathering of the church (10:25). Some already had withdrawn from the faith (6:4–8), and all were in danger of committing apostasy (3:12)—which seems to imply a defection to Judaism (13:9–14).

STUDY QUESTION 6

We can only speculate concerning the identity of the author of Hebrews and its destination. What is indicated about Paul as a possible author in Hebrews 2:3? What may Hebrews 13:24 indicate about its destination?

Two passages are extremely important in regard to the author and the destination of Hebrews. Many scholars point to Heb. 2:3 as evidence that Paul was not the author, for the writer seems to include himself among those who heard the Gospel secondhand—an admission that goes directly against the claim of Paul (Gal. 1:1, 12; 1 Cor. 9:1; 11:23; 15:8; Eph. 3:3). The other passage is "Those from Italy greet you" (13:24). It may imply that some Christians from Italy (or Rome) are with the author and are sending greetings to their friends at Rome. The intended readers, therefore, may be some of the household churches at Rome (cf. Rom. 16:5, 14, 15). This proposal fits the historical fact that Hebrews was known to the early church fathers at Rome, Clement and Hermas.

Possible Answers

Concerning authorship we must admit that, in the words of Origen, "only God knows." A good guess, however, might be Apollos, for the content and style of Hebrews agree extremely well with what we are told about Apollos, an Alexandrian Jew who was eloquent and well versed in the Scriptures (Acts 18:24–28). But the deduction is merely a guess.

The destination of Hebrews may be one or several of the house churches in Rome, as suggested above. References to persecution would lend support to this deduction and would tend to place the date of composition around the time of the persecution of Christians by Nero.

The danger confronting the addressees seems to be a relapse into Judaism, for the argument of Hebrews as a whole is that Christianity is far superior to Judaism and supersedes it.

Putting together the available evidence and attempting only *probable* answers, we might consider the following situation as a possibility—and merely a possibility:

The addressees belong to Jewish Christian assemblies at Rome. A prior persecution had occurred under the emperor Claudius in A.D. 49 (Acts 18:2). Under Nero Christianity again became a persecuted religion (A.D. 64–65). Nero's fury first fell on Gentile Christians at Rome. The Jewish Christians had sympathy for their suffering brethren and attempted to help them. Although martyrdom had not yet extended to the Jewish Christians, they realized that the danger was ever present. Their temptation, therefore, was to minimize their Christian characteristics and to emphasize their Jewish background—to conceal their Christian faith under the guise of Judaism. Such a position of compromise caused a spiritual dullness and a danger of a relapse into Judaism.

STUDY QUESTION 7

Hebrews stresses the superiority of Christ as our High Priest. To whom is He superior according to Hebrews 1:1–3; 1:4–2:18; 3:1–6? See also Hebrews 4:14–5:4; 8:1–6.

Content of Hebrews

The content of Hebrews centers on the person and work of Jesus Christ. It begins with a superb statement on the deity of Christ. Through Him God has made His supreme and final revelation to human beings. Christ is far above the angels, who worship Him (chap. 1). He is also the Son of Man, who suffered and died for all people, thus atoning for their sins (chap. 2). He is superior to Moses (chap. 3) and is our great High Priest, superior also to Melchizedek (chap. 4–6). Through our new High Priest we have a new covenant, for Jesus offered Himself as the one final sacrifice, far superior to the animal sacrifices in the Old Testament (chap. 7–10).

Faith is confident reliance on God's Word and certainty about future unseen realities, as numerous examples in the Old Testament testify (chap. 11). These great heroes of faith are watching us, an incentive to us to persevere in the face of suffering (chap. 12). We must make a choice between a code of religious observances and the salvation offered by Jesus Christ (chap. 13).

Outline of Hebrews

I. Christ is superior to
   A. the prophets (1:1–3);
   B. the angels (1:4–2:18);
   C. Moses (3:1–6).
      (Warning about unbelief, 3:7–4:13)
II. Christ's priesthood is superior to the Levitical priesthood (4:14–7:28).
III. Christ's sacrifice is superior to the animal sacrifices by the Levitical priests (8:1–10:39).
IV. The triumphs of faith (11:1–40)
V. The application to the present trials (12:1–29)
VI. Admonition and conclusion (13:1–25)
   (Other warnings are inserted at 5:11–6:20; 10:26–39; 12:18–29.)

15. *Letters of Peter and Jude: God's Grace in Trials*

*T*he letters of Peter and Jude are written to the people of God who are faced with various trials. In 1 Peter the trials are primarily various persecutions; in 2 Peter and Jude the trials consist mainly in temptations from false doctrine and false teachers.

1 Peter

Peter, the author, was one of the leading disciples of Jesus and the chief spokesman at Pentecost. After being miraculously released from prison (Acts 12:1–19), he may have gone to Antioch in Syria (Gal. 2:11) and was back in Jerusalem for the Apostolic Council (Acts 15:6–14). We cannot be certain of the details of his travels. Either he or some of his converts showed up at Corinth (1 Cor. 1:12). Tradition places him at Rome in the latter part of his life, from where he no doubt wrote 1 Peter.

STUDY QUESTION 1

Who are the addressees of 1 Peter?

A. *To which five provinces was 1 Peter sent? See 1 Peter 1:1. Which of these were represented at Pentecost? See Acts 2:9.*

B. *What does 1 Peter 1:12 indicate about the founders of the church in this area? Were these people pri-*

marily Jews or Gentiles? See 1 Peter 1:14; 2:10; 4:3–4.

Addressees of 1 Peter

The addressees of 1 Peter resided in five Roman provinces in northern Asia Minor (modern Turkey). Acts does not mention any travels of Peter in this area. It does list, however, three of the provinces (Cappadocia, Pontus, Asia) as being represented at Pentecost (Acts 2:9). It is very possible, therefore, that the origin of these churches stems from Pentecost rather than from a visit of Peter to these regions. In fact, there is no indication in 1 Peter that he founded these churches or that he was even personally acquainted with them. Note that Peter refers to "those who have preached the Gospel to you" (1:12); he does not say "we who have preached the Gospel to you."

From 1 Peter it seems clear that the addressees were of Gentile background. Peter refers to "the former lusts, as in your ignorance" (1:14). He also calls them people "who once were not a people but are now the people of God, who had not obtained mercy but now have obtained mercy" (2:10). Peter further urges: "We have spent enough of our past lifetime in doing the will of the Gentiles" (4:3) and then lists various sins of the Gentiles, including idolatry (4:3–4). While there no doubt were also Jewish Christians in this area, the Gentiles seem to be the predominant part.

STUDY QUESTION 2

What is the situation of the Christians? See 1 Peter 1:6–7; 3:16–17; 4:4, 14, 16; 2:13–17. What is Peter's encouragement? See 1 Peter 1:3–7; 2:12; 4:5; 5:12.

The Occasion for 1 Peter

The addressees are experiencing some type of persecution or harassment (1:6–7; 3:16–17). They are being slandered, ridiculed, and suspected of disloyalty to the government (4:4, 14, 16; 2:13–17). Yet we do not read of a full-scale official persecution for refusing to worship the emperor or one that resulted in the confiscation of property, imprisonment, or martyrdom—even though Peter refers to a "fiery trial which is to try you" (4:12).

Peter is encouraging the readers to show endurance and to stand fast in their faith (5:9–12). In Christian hope they must look beyond the condemnation by humans to the judgment of God. From human beings they may suffer grief, but their Christian hope will be vindicated when Christ comes as the final judge (1:3–7). In human courts they may be accused, but God will be glorified "in the day of visitation" (2.12). Pagan neighbors may heap abuse on them now, but these same people "will give an account to Him who is ready to judge the living and the dead" (4:5). Christians, therefore, although now persecuted unjustly, can hope to be vindicated before the judgment throne of God.

STUDY QUESTION 3

What three figurative terms are used in 1 Peter 5:13? How may this verse help indicate the time and place of 1 Peter? What does church tradition state about Peter's last days?

Time and Place of 1 Peter

A key passage is at the end of 1 Peter: "She who is in Babylon, elect together with you, greets you; and so does Mark my son" (5:13). This verse seems to be using figurative language. We know that Mark was not Peter's physical son but rather his "son" in the faith. So "son" is used figuratively. The word "she" also seems to be used figuratively, referring to the church (which is feminine in Greek) rather than to some lady or to Peter's wife. Furthermore, "Babylon" has a symbolic background. In Old Testament prophecy "Babylon" denoted a secular power that was an enemy of God's people. Christianity adopted this word to denote its adversary, as we see from several passages in Revelation (14.8; 16:19; 17:5; 18:2). Thus Peter for some reason seems to be using "Babylon" as a figurative term for a secular power that is opposing God's people. Since tradition places Peter at Rome in his later years, he no doubt uses "Babylon" as a figurative term for Rome.

The exact time of composition is not certain. Some date 1 Peter during the Neronian persecution on the basis of the phrase "if anyone suffers as a Christian" (4:16). Others prefer to date it before the persecution by Nero, since Peter urges his readers to be loyal to the government (2:13–17). It is also possible—in fact, very probable—that while persecution by Nero was confined to Rome, Peter is warning the readers in Asia Minor in case it should spread there—and therefore he is using the symbolic term "Babylon" in case the document should fall into the wrong hands.

In brief, 1 Peter seems to have been composed at Rome in the mid-sixties.

Content of 1 Peter

1 Peter begins by stressing the hope Christians have even in times of suffering, while undergoing tests of their faith. The present brief period of trials will be overshadowed by the future, when believers will come into their promised inheritance. They will experience supreme joy at the coming of Christ, the foundation of their salvation. At present they should model their behavior on the pattern of Christ and live in holiness (chap. 1).

In their lives Christians should reflect that they are God's people, a chosen race and a holy nation. The world sees God as He is reflected in the lives of His people. Although Christians are suspect as aliens in the world, they must endure such accusations and be obedient to civil authorities. In all their relationships they are to respect authority—especially in the relationships between servants and masters and between wives and husbands. Love, respect, and consideration are to be the marks of Christians. As Noah was saved by the ark floating on water, so the water of Baptism saves believers and cleanses them from sin (chap. 2–3).

Christians are to be ready when trials come and are to suffer joyfully for the cause of Christ. As glory for Christ followed His suffering, so the trials of Christians are a prelude to their glory. The end of all things is at hand; therefore, Christians should continue in prayer, show love for one another, and practice hospitality. In everything God should be glorified—even by rejoicing in sharing Christ's sufferings (chap. 4).

Peter appeals to the leaders to tend God's flock as true shepherds, exhibiting a wholesome example. He also appeals to the members to be subject to the leaders by showing humility to them and to one another. All are to be watchful against the opposition of the devil. In their sufferings God will strengthen them and finally call them to eternal glory (chap. 5).

Outline of 1 Peter

I. Greetings (1:1–2)
II. Hope through Christ (1:3–12)
III. Hope with holiness of life (1:13–2:10)
IV. Hope in spite of suffering (2:11–4:11)
V. Advice for the persecuted (4:12–5:11)
VI. Conclusion (5:12–14)

Comment

Some see in the first part of 1 Peter an address delivered to those who were just baptized into the Christian faith (1:3–4:11) and in the second section a message to the whole church. Be that as it may, 1 Peter is one of the richest theological documents in the New Testament, meriting most careful study.

---

2 Peter

While 1 Peter treats God's grace in trials of persecution, 2 Peter deals with God's grace in trials resulting from false teaching. Although both epistles were written by the same author, the difference in subject suggests that 2 Peter should be studied in connection with Jude, which deals with the same type of false teaching exposed in 2 Peter. In fact, some historical questions concerning 2 Peter are better answered when discussed simultaneously with the Epistle of Jude.

STUDY QUESTION 4

Was 2 Peter written to the same addressees as 1 Peter? See 2 Peter 3:1; compare 1 Peter 1:1 and 2 Peter 1:1; compare 2 Peter 1:16 and 1 Peter 1:12.

Historical Questions

It is usually assumed that 2 Peter is written to the same addressees as 1 Peter, the Christians in five Roman provinces of Asia

Minor (modern Turkey). The main reason for this assumption is the statement: "Beloved, I now write to you this second epistle" (2 Peter 3:1). However, it should be noted that in its greeting 2 Peter does not claim to be addressing the five provinces but has the general statement: "To those who have obtained like precious faith with us" (2 Peter 1:1; cf. 1 Peter 1:1). It is not proven, therefore, that both epistles by Peter are written to the same readers. In 2 Peter the author refers to himself in the Greek text as "Simeon Peter" (1:1). Simeon, or Simon, was his original Jewish name. It is likely that Peter uses this form of his name in 2 Peter because he is addressing Jewish Christians—possibly at some place in Palestine. We should note that James in Jerusalem refers to Peter as Simon (Acts 15:14). Also pertinent is Peter's apparent personal acquaintance with the addressees of 2 Peter, for he refers to the time "when we made known to you the power and coming of our Lord Jesus Christ" (1:16). It seems that others, not Peter, preached the Good News to the addressees of 1 Peter (1:12). In any event, the destination of 2 Peter must remain an open historical question.

The reason for this lack of clarity may be the fact that 2 Peter has the least external evidence of all the documents in the New Testament. Only after several centuries is there a clear statement in the church fathers that 2 Peter was written by the apostle Peter. There may be two reasons for such a late identification of the author. First, in the early church several documents claiming Peter as the author clearly were forgeries. There was a "Gospel of Peter," a "Preaching of Peter," an "Acts of Peter," and a "Revelation of Peter." The circulation of these forgeries made the early church fathers extremely cautious about accepting any document claiming to be by Peter into the New Testament canon. Thus the early church wisely was not gullible but acknowledged the genuineness of 2 Peter only after long and careful scrutiny.

The second reason is that several genuine documents addressed originally to Jewish Christians were also questioned during some periods of the early church. After the church became extensively a Gentile church, epistles originally written to Jewish Christians apparently were not used as much. Examples are James, Hebrews, and Jude. If 2 Peter was written for Jewish Christians in Palestine (and not to the same people as 1 Peter), it would also fall under this category and tend to be neglected in the early church. At least there are valid reasons for the late recognition of 2 Peter as a canonical book.

Also pertinent to the relationship between 1 Peter and 2 Peter is the remark that Peter wrote 1 Peter "by Silvanus" (1 Peter 5:12). Since the Greek of 1 Peter is so superior to that of 2 Peter, this remark may indicate that Silvanus was more than a secretary; he probably polished the Greek of 1 Peter, and thus its literary style would naturally be superior to that of 2 Peter, in which Silvanus is not mentioned, and which Peter probably composed himself.

Because these historical questions must remain open, we should not try to be dogmatic in determining the destination of 2 Peter nor its time and place of writing.

STUDY QUESTION 5

What is the situation of the Christians in 2 Peter? See 2 Peter 2:10, 13, 18; 2:3, 14, 15. What warnings does Peter give in 2 Peter 2?

The Occasion for 2 Peter

The primary occasion for the writing of 2 Peter is the presence of false teachers in some areas of the church. Their false teaching is dealt with mainly in the second chapter. Peter refers to their licentiousness (2:2 in the Greek and 2:18), their lust of defiling passion (2:10), their reveling and carousing (2:13), and their eyes full of adultery (2:14). Greed is another of their sins (2:3, 14, 15). They also despise authority (2:10). According to the last chapter the false teachers were also denying the certainty of Christ's return (3:3–13).

Frequently the terms "libertine" and "antinomian" are used to describe this type of false teaching. Libertine refers to an attitude that Christians are at liberty to live any way they wish. Morality becomes a matter of personal choice because God's gracious forgiveness is interpreted to grant liberty from the demands of the Law and to allow freedom to live as one pleases. Antinomian describes the same attitude. It means "against law" and presents the view that God's grace gives Christians license to live as they wish. The false premise of the libertines or antinomians fails to see that Christ freed us *from* sin and not *to* sin, in order that we might live to His glory and not according to our sinful natural passion.

Content of 2 Peter

Peter stresses first that we should become like Christ and that our spiritual growth depends on knowledge, which results in deeds. Peter, like James, insists that genuine faith cannot be separated from a holy life. The good news of the Gospel rests on the evidence of eyewitnesses, not on myth. Peter testifies that he was with Jesus on the mountain of transfiguration (chap. 1).

Then Peter warns against the libertine or antinomian false teachers. They respect no authority and teach self-gratification, denying the Lord and shaming the church. They will be punished, as were others in the Old Testament—e.g., the fallen angels, the evil world at the time of Noah, and the cities of Sodom and Gomorrah. Peter continues the description of the false teachers (chap. 2).

Finally Peter discusses the second coming of Christ—a teaching probably also scoffed at by the false teachers. The flood at the time of Noah is an example of God's sudden action. The end of the world will come just as unexpectedly, as a thief in the night. But this time destruction will be by fire, not by water. It is pertinent to note the striking relevance of Peter's description of the destruction of the world in an age that fears multimegaton atomic bombs. For Christians Christ's second coming will result in "new heavens and a new earth in which righteousness dwells" (chap. 3).

Outline of 2 Peter

I. True knowledge (chap. 1)
II. False teachers (chap. 2)
III. Christ's return (chap. 3)

Jude

The close parallelism between Jude and 2 Peter 2 makes it logical to treat these two epistles in the same chapter.

STUDY QUESTION 6

What do we know about Jude (Judas), the brother of James? See Mark 6:3; Matt. 13:55; 1 Cor. 9:5. Why he

does not call himself a "brother of Jesus Christ" in Jude 1 may be explained by Matt. 12:46–50.

Author of Jude

The author of this document of 25 verses refers to himself as "Jude, a servant of Jesus Christ, and brother of James" (v. 1) but does not call himself an apostle. Since he speaks of the apostles as "they" (vv. 17–18), it seems clear that he is not the apostle Judas mentioned in Luke 6:16. He must be one of the Lord's brothers listed in Mark 6:3 and Matthew 13:55 (where the alternate spelling "Judas" appears) and mentioned in Acts 1:14. These brothers had not believed in Jesus during His earthly ministry. No doubt they came to faith after Jesus' resurrection, when He appeared to James (1 Cor. 15:7). Apparently they were active in missionary work (1 Cor. 9:5). The brother James is prominent in the Apostolic Council (Acts 15) and is called a "pillar" of the Jerusalem church (Gal. 2:9). It is this James, we believe, who wrote the Epistle of James. His brother, Jude, composed the short letter under discussion.

At first it may seem surprising that he calls himself not a "brother of Jesus Christ" but a "servant of Jesus Christ" (v. 1). Possibly he recalled what Jesus said when told that His brothers were waiting to speak with Him. Jesus stretched out His hand toward His disciples and said: "Here are My mother and My brothers! For whoever does the will of My Father in heaven is My brother and sister and mother" (Matt. 12:49–50). His own experience taught Jude that faith, not kinship, bound him to Jesus. His new relationship with the Christ overshadowed any regard for family ties.

Addressees of Jude

We cannot be certain about the destination of this letter since Jude and the other brothers apparently did some traveling in promoting missionary endeavors (1 Cor. 9:5). But a few facts should be mentioned. James, his brother, was highly esteemed particularly by Jewish Christians, and Jude does identify himself to his readers as "brother of James." He also uses Jewish illustrations and Jewish tradition. These facts may indicate that he is addressing Jewish Christians. But their location must remain an open question.

Date of Jude

The date of composition, furthermore, cannot be determined with any precision, for we do not know how long Jude lived. It is highly unlikely, however, that he wrote after the destruction of Jerusalem in A.D. 70. He does refer to other examples of destruction that befell the ungodly. If the fall of Jerusalem had already occurred, it is difficult to see how he could have omitted mention of this event as a prime example of divine judgment on the faithless. But again, the question of date must remain open, for arguments from silence frequently are not strong.

STUDY QUESTION 7

What similarity is there between Jude's references to noncanonical sources (vv. 9, 14–15) and Paul's use of them in Acts 17:28 and 2 Tim. 3:8?

References to Noncanonical Sources

Twice Jude refers to noncanonical sources—citing the Book of Enoch (vv. 14–15) and referring to the content of the Assumption of Moses (v. 9)—Jewish documents not included in the Old Testament canon. Such books are also called apocryphal or pseudepigrapha. At first it may seem strange to find such references in a New Testament document. But we must remember that Jude is not putting any stamp of approval on these two documents as if they should be regarded as equal in authority to the canonical Old and New Testament. No doubt he is citing them because the false teachers against whom he is writing frequently appealed to these works, and thus he is turning the tables on them. His references to noncanonical sources is no more strange than Paul's references to heathen poets (Acts 17:28) and to noncanonical sources in order to supply the names of two magicians not recorded in the Old Testament (2 Tim. 3:8).

The only deduction we should draw is that these bits of historical information, although derived from noncanonical sources, are true, not that the noncanonical sources themselves are inspired.

STUDY QUESTION 8

What parallel warnings against false teachers do we find in Jude and 2 Peter 2?

Jude and 2 Peter 2

Most interesting and unique is the parallelism between the false teachers in Jude and those in 2 Peter 2, as it may be outlined in the following table:

Jude	Parallels	2 Peter 2
4	Denying Christ	1–3
6	Evil angels	4
7	Sodom and Gomorrah	6
8	Defile/authority/revile	10
9	Reviling accusation	11
10	Brute beasts	12
11	Balaam	15
12–13	Spots/without water	13–17
16	Great swelling words	18

It should be observed that the parallels are not only similar in content but also occur in virtually the same order in Jude and 2 Peter 2. It seems clear that one of these authors had the work of the other before him when he composed his document. But whose work came first and whose was second?

This is another question that cannot be answered with certainty. Several points, however, favor the conclusion that Peter wrote first and that Jude, with Peter's permission, followed the content and the order of Peter's second chapter. Some scholars point out that it is more likely for the more obscure Jude to cite the "apostolic" Peter than the reverse. Others note that Peter at times uses the future tense in describing the false teachers (2 Peter 2:1–3), while Jude never uses the future tense; hence, Jude seems to follow Peter. Also, in the opinion of some, Jude 17–18 may be a reference to 2 Peter 3:3, thus indicating that Jude should be placed after 2 Peter. It should be mentioned furthermore that 2 Peter does not show any evidence of "seams," as we would expect if Peter sandwiched the material he adapted from Jude between his other material.

In brief, it is possible—perhaps even probable, although not definitely certain—that Peter wrote 2 Peter letter for specific churches where he had worked, warning them against false teachers. At the same time Jude, who was aware of Peter's composition, was faced with the same type of false teachers already active in churches where he had labored. Jude then received permission from Peter to incorporate a portion of 2 Peter in writing to his constituency. Such a situation is at least a reasonable probability. That would make 2 Peter the earliest cited document in the New Testament rather than the latest work quoted by the church fathers—assuming, of course, that Jude 17–18 refers to 2 Peter 3:3.

The Occasion for Jude

Apparently the false teachers described in Jude were of a similar stripe to those discussed in 2 Peter—libertines or antinomians, people who interpreted God's grace as freedom *to* sin, not as freedom *from* sin. Jude calls them "ungodly" and "licentious" people, who "deny the only Lord God and our Lord Jesus Christ" (v. 4). They are immoral (vv. 7, 16), reject authority (v. 8), are greedy (v. 16), and create divisions in the church (v. 19).

These false teachers were working within the church, having gained admission secretly (v. 4), and were present at the common meals of the church (v. 12). Jude compares them with clouds (from which people expect beneficial rain), to trees (from which people expect fruit), and to stars (from which sailors expect guidance). But Jude calls them *waterless* clouds, *fruitless* trees, and *wandering* stars (vv. 12–13)—that is, they set themselves up as leaders but are misleading their followers.

Content of Jude

Jude describes the false teachers mentioned above and assures the church that they are doomed by God to destruction, just as God acted in similar instances in history. For example, God punished Sodom and Gomorrah for sexual immorality (Gen. 19), Cain for murdering his brother (Gen. 4), Balaam for betraying his position as a prophet (Num. 31:8, 16), and Korah for his rebellion against God (Num. 16).

The church must resist such false teachers by growing in faith, by prayer, and with the help of the Holy Spirit. For God is able to keep them from falling away.

Outline of Jude

I. Greeting (vv. 1–2)
II. Purpose of Letter (vv. 3–4)
III. Examples of God's judgment (vv. 5–7)

16. *John's Gospel and Epistles: God's Grace and the Beloved Disciple*

John's Gospel

The main reason for discussing John's gospel at this point rather than after Matthew, Mark, and Luke is that John's approach is different from the other three gospels, which are called synoptics because they have a similar portrayal of Jesus' earthly ministry and His person. Although John presents the same truth as the other three, he does so in a different way and in greater depth. He records events in Jesus' life, as do the synoptics, but he frequently also interprets them. He uses figurative terms taken from common experience (bread, water, light, life, door, shepherd) as well as contrasting concepts (light/darkness, love/hatred) to interpret the meaning of Jesus.

Author

The author of the Fourth Gospel does not mention himself by name, but he refers to himself as "the disciple whom Jesus loved" (21:20–24; cf. 13:23; 19:26; 20:2; 21:7). Early church tradition agrees that the author is John the apostle, the brother of James and son of Zebedee (Mark 1:19–20). Not only does John never mention himself by name, but he also never mentions his brother, James, by name. The brothers are referred to once as "the sons of Zebedee" (21:2). Yet John does supply the names of all the other apostles who appear in his gospel. These facts may indicate that John the apostle is the author and that he purposely refuses to mention himself or his brother by name in order to avoid appearing to enhance his reputation or that of his brother.

No doubt a relatively young man during Jesus' ministry, John was the only disciple present at Jesus' crucifixion and was entrusted with the care of His mother Mary (19:25–27). John began to follow Jesus after a miraculous catch of fish (Luke 5:1–11), and after a similar miracle it was John who recognized the presence of the resurrected Lord (21:4–7). He may have been Jesus' cousin, his mother Salome being the sister of Mary (cf. Matt. 27:56; Mark 15:40; John 19:25). John, James, and Peter were the leaders of the 12 disciples and were permitted to see Jesus' transfiguration (Matt. 17:1–8; Mark 9:2–8; Luke 9:28–36).

John had a fruitful ministry both in Palestine and later in Asia Minor. Soon after Jesus' ascension John and Peter healed a lame man at the temple in Jerusalem (Acts 3:1–26). As a result of this miracle, they had to defend themselves before the Jewish Sanhedrin (4:1–22). After the message of the Good News spread to Samaria, the church at Jerusalem sent John with Peter to investigate the situation there (8:14–17). Paul speaks of John as one of the pillars of the Jerusalem church (Gal. 2:9). According to early church tradition John later went to Asia Minor (modern Turkey) and settled at Ephesus. This tradition is substantiated in the book of Revelation, which associates John with seven churches in Asia Minor and with the neighboring island of Patmos (Rev. 1:4, 9, 11). No doubt these seven churches of Asia Minor also were the recipients of John's gospel.

STUDY QUESTION 1

Many students of Scripture believe that John wrote his gospel to a church in conflict.

A. **What conflict may be indicated in John 5:18; 8:39–44; 16:2? But note also 4:22; 11:49–51; 19:19.**

B. **What conflict may be indicated in John 1:6–8; 1:19–23; 1:29–36; 3:28–30? Note also Acts 19:1–7; 18:24–26.**

C. **What conflict may be indicated in 1:1–3; 1:14; 1:29; 19:34; 20:27–28? Note also 1 John 5:6.**

Occasion

John states the occasion and purpose of his gospel very clearly: "Truly Jesus did many other signs in the presence of His disciples, which are not written in this book; but these are written that you may believe that Jesus is the Christ, the Son of God, and that believing you may have life in His name" (20:30–31). This statement seems to indicate that John is addressing Christian churches in order to bolster their faith in Jesus as the Messiah and the Son of God.

From the first three chapters of Revelation we know that there were problems in the churches in Asia Minor. From certain indications in John's gospel these churches appear to have had conflicts both within and without. One of the conflicts apparently was with the surrounding unbelieving Jews, for John depicts the situation in language even stronger than Matthew. In John's gospel the term "Jew" is equivalent to "unbelieving Jew." The Jews deny that Jesus is the Son of God and seek to kill Him (5:18). They act as children of the devil (8:39–44) and are fulfilling Jesus' prediction of continued opposition to Christianity (16:2).

But John is not anti-Semitic. His harsh words also are a call to repentance. John reminds his readers that "salvation is of the Jews" (4:22). The high priest of the Jews, according to John, refers to Jesus as dying also for their nation (11:49–51). In John's gospel Jesus is called "the King of Israel" (1:49) and "the King of the Jews" (19:19). Some scholars, therefore, regard John's gospel primarily as a missionary appeal to the Jewish people.

Another conflict facing the churches in Asia Minor seems to have involved the followers of John the Baptist, who apparently continued to exist as a separate sect and had spread by the mid-fifties to Ephesus (Acts 19:1–7), where John probably wrote his gospel. We know that a similar sect exists even today along the Euphrates River, claiming to follow John the Baptist. Such loyalty to John the Baptist no doubt continued to exist at Ephesus in the mid-nineties. This situation explains why John emphasizes that the forerunner John the Baptist is subordinate to Jesus: "He was not that Light, but was sent to bear witness of that Light" (1:8). He was not the Christ but merely a voice crying in the wilderness (1:19–23). John the Baptist himself declares that he must decrease while Jesus increases (3:28–30) and points to Jesus as the Lamb of God who takes away the sin of the world (1:29–36).

A third conflict facing the church around Ephesus involved an early heresy developed by a certain Cerinthus. Known as Gnosti- cism, it was based on a belief in a radical dualism between material and spiritual elements. This false teaching assumed that everything consisting of matter—physical objects—was essentially evil but that everything spiritual—nonmaterial—was good. These Gnostics, therefore, had a problem explaining how a good God could create a physical or material universe. They tried to solve it by denying the creation account in Genesis and by supposing that some inferior deities were responsible for the existence of the material universe. To counteract this heresy John is very decisive at the beginning of his gospel. He states that in the beginning Jesus, called the Word, was with God, was God, and took an active part in creation—in fact, nothing was made without Him (1:1–3).

The Gnostics also had a problem with the person of Jesus Christ. They could not comprehend, according to their basic dualism, how a deity (spiritual) could become flesh and blood (material). They tried to solve their problem by denying that the incarnation of Jesus ever took place. Therefore they distinguished between Jesus and Christ. They taught that Jesus was born a natural human being with a physical body. At His baptism the heavenly Christ took possession of Jesus and endowed Him with power to perform miracles. But shortly before His death on the cross the heavenly Christ left Him. Only the human Jesus died, just as only the human Jesus was born. Jesus' words, "My God, My God, why have You forsaken Me?" (Matt. 27:46; Mark 15:34) were interpreted by the Gnostics as "My power, My power, why have you left me?"—as if at that moment the heavenly Christ left the human Jesus so that only a human being died on the cross.

It is noteworthy to see how John's gospel counteracts the false teaching of the Gnostics. John clearly states: "The Word became flesh" (1:14). He relates that John the Baptist referred to Jesus as the Lamb of God, that is, as the Christ being sacrificed for the sins of the world and dying on the cross (1:29). Then at the end of the gospel, Thomas refers to the resurrected Jesus as "My Lord and my God" (20:27–28). John also relates that blood and water flowed from Jesus' side (19:34)—water in which Jesus once was baptized and blood caused by His crucifixion—implying that the same Jesus Christ who was present at His baptism also died on the cross. (This implication is clearer from 1 John 5:6).

STUDY QUESTION 2

Church tradition claims that John wrote his gospel around A.D. 90–100 to the churches in Asia Minor (see Rev. 1:4, 11).

A. *Compare the content of John with that of the synoptics (Matthew, Mark, Luke). Which accounts overlap? Which accounts does John omit?*

B. *How does Jesus' style of teaching in John compare with His style of teaching in the synoptics? Note "signs," figurative language, long discourses, "sevens," Passovers. Compare John 19:13–14 with Mark 15:25. How could "sixth hour" precede "third hour"?*

C. *Are there any clues to indicate that the addressees of John's gospel were acquainted with the synoptics?*

Date and Place

Although not all students agree on the date and place of the writing of John's gospel—some preferring to put it before A.D. 70—the evidence discussed above supports the view that John wrote around A.D. 90–100 at Ephesus for the church there and for other surrounding congregations. The evidence is basically twofold: (1) the information about John in the first three chapters of Revelation, which connect him with the churches of Asia Minor; (2) church tradition, which corroborates the information of Revelation and which dates the heresy of Cerinthus in the last years of the first century A.D.

This date for John's gospel (A.D. 90–100) would place it later than the three synoptic gospels of Matthew, Mark, and Luke. Are there any clues in John's gospel (when compared with the synoptics) that substantiate a date for John later than for Matthew, Mark, and Luke? We feel that at least two clues are pertinent to this question. One is the fact that John does not list the names of the 12 disciples, while their names are given in Matthew, Mark, and Luke. The reason for John's omission could be that he did not think such a list would be important. Or John could have omitted the list because he was writing to Christians who already had this information in the synoptics—and the repetition in his judgment would have been unnecessary.

The other clue comes from a comparison of the content of John's gospel with that of the three synoptics. In most cases an event described in one of the three synoptics appears also in another or in all three. For this reason, Matthew, Mark, and Luke are taken together in studying the ministry of Jesus. But John's gospel is quite unique in content. Besides the account of Jesus' death and resurrection, it contains only two incidents that the synoptics also report: the feeding of the five thousand (6:1–14) and Jesus' walking on the lake (6:15–21). All the other accounts of Jesus' career as told by John are found only in his gospel. Why this selectivity of John? It is reasonable to assume that he wrote later than the synoptics and knew that his readers already possessed Matthew, Mark, and Luke. John, therefore, did not wish to repeat what the other three had written. As an aged disciple—the last one still alive—he purposely omitted the bulk of the synoptic gospels (except the Passion and resurrection, which could not be left out) and emphasized other events in Jesus' ministry that he considered important for the church to know.

John and the Synoptics

We have already referred to several differences between John and the synoptics—his content, his interpretation of events, and his use of symbolic language. Now we shall discuss other unique aspects.

John's gospel contains no parables. Jesus, however, does engage in long discourses. John does not refer to Jesus' superhuman acts as miracles but as "signs," thus stressing what they *signified*. He is partial to the number "seven." He includes seven signs:

1. Wine at Cana (2:1–12)
2. Healing of nobleman's son (4:46–54)
3. Healing of man at pool of Bethesda (5:1–9)
4. Feeding of five thousand (6:1–14)
5. Walking on lake (6:15–21)
6. Healing of blind man (9:1–7)
7. Raising of Lazarus (11:38–44).

Jesus refers to Himself as "I am" in seven accounts:

1. Bread of life (6:25–58)
2. Light of the world (8:12)
3. Good Shepherd (10:1–18)
4. Door (10:1–18)

5. Resurrection and Life (11:25)
6. Way, Truth, and Life (14:6)
7. True Vine (15:1–8)

John reports that the beginning of Jesus' ministry took place in a seven-day period: "next day," or second day (1:29); "next day," or third day (1:35); "following day," or fourth day (1:43); "third day" (following), or seventh day (2:1). Some also see a seven-day account in John's Passion narrative. The stress on the number "seven," of course, reminds us of its frequent occurrence in John's Revelation.

Another distinctive feature of John's gospel is its chronology. Only John reports the early Judean ministry of Jesus, devoting the first chapters to a period not mentioned by the synoptics during which Jesus moved freely between Judea and Galilee. He speaks of three Passovers (2:13; 6:4; 13:1), while the synoptics mention only the Passover when Jesus was crucified. He apparently uses the Roman time frame (a new day beginning at midnight), while the synoptics use Jewish reckoning (a new daylight period being calculated from 6:00 a.m.). Thus Jesus is before Pilate at 6:00 a.m. or "the sixth hour" in Roman reckoning (John 19:13–14) and is crucified at 9:00 a.m. or "the third hour" in Jewish reckoning (Mark 15:25).

Also distinctive in John's gospel is the openness with which Jesus speaks about Himself, while in the synoptics He is reluctant to confess His identity. John also frequently links Jesus' teaching to His wondrous deeds. While all four gospels relate the feeding of the five thousand, for example, only in John does Jesus describe Himself the next day as the Bread of life (6:1–59). He proclaims that He is the Light of the world in connection with His opening the eyes of a blind person (8:12–9:41). He asserts that He is the Resurrection and the Life when He raises Lazarus from the dead (11:17–44).

Finally, John omits many events recorded in the synoptics. Some of these are most important in the life and ministry of Jesus— His birth, baptism (only alluded to in 1:29–34), temptation by the devil, transfiguration, institution of the Lord's Supper, agony in Gethsemane. These omissions are understandable if, as we have suggested, John is writing later in the first century for Christians who are acquainted with Matthew, Mark, and Luke, which gospels do include the important events omitted by John.

STUDY QUESTION 3

Match four statements in John's prologue (1:11a; 1:11b; 1:12; 1:16) with their elaborations in the four main sections of the Gospel—chapters 1–4; 5–12; 13–17; 18–20.

Content of John

The content of John exhibits a very logical structure. The first section of 18 verses, called the prolog, describes Jesus as the Word of God in the flesh, the Word that His own people would not heed.

This Word is spoken to Israel. John the Baptist bears witness to Jesus. The early disciples confess His identity. A miracle or "sign" shows Jesus' power. He cleanses the temple. The interview with Nicodemus teaches that people need a spiritual birth. John the Baptist steps down. Jesus meets a Samaritan woman at a well. He performs a second "sign" by healing a son of an official. This activity takes place all over the area—in Judea, Samaria, and Galilee (1.19–4.54)

In the next section Jesus, the Word, is rejected by Israel. The Jews are estranged from God. All forsake Jesus except the 12 disciples. Some Jews seek to stone Him. Jesus proclaims a judgment on the unbelievers and brands teachers who oppose Him as false. Some Jews regard Jesus as blasphemous. The Jewish leaders decide that He must die. The chief priests and Pharisees are hardened against Him (5:1–12:50).

The third section describes the relationship between Jesus and the disciples. Jesus elaborates for them His commandment on love. He promises them the Holy Spirit for guidance and prays His high-priestly prayer (13:1–17:26).

The last section concerns God's grace and truth through Jesus' crucifixion and resurrection, which culminate in His glory (18:1–20.31).

Finally, John adds an appendix (chap. 21) in which Jesus appears in Galilee and converses with Peter and John.

Outline of John

I. Prolog (1:1–18)
II. The Word spoken to Israel (1:19–4:54)
III. The Word rejected by Israel (5:1–12:50)
IV. The Word received by the disciples (13:1–17:26)
V. The Word of God speaks grace and truth (18:1–20:31)
VI. Appendix (21:1–25)

A comparison of the four main sections of this outline with the prolog reveals another distinctive characteristic in John's gospel: the material is arranged in a spiral movement. That is, several statements in the prolog give clues to the content of a section in the general outline of the gospel. John's spiral movement may be illustrated in the following table:

Section	Clue in Prolog
The Word spoken to Israel	"He came to His own" (1:11a)
The Word rejected by Israel	"His own did not receive Him" (1:11b)
The Word received by disciples	"But as many as received Him, to them He gave the right to become children of God" (1:12)
The Word speaks grace and truth	"And of His fullness we have all received, and grace for grace" (1:16)

A similar spiral movement, we shall see, characterizes other writings of John—1 John and Revelation.

---

1 John

On the basis of the language, style, and content, as well as the evidence of early church tradition, the author of 1 John is the same as the author of the Fourth Gospel—the apostle John. The content also seems to have a close relationship with the other two epistles of John.

Although 1 John does not have the usual epistolary beginning or ending, we include it among the letters because of its references to writing (1:4; 2:1, 7–8, 12–14, 21, 26; 5:13), but some prefer to

196

regard it as a homily or sermon. While Hebrews does not have the usual epistolary beginning and James omits the usual epistolary ending, 1 John omits both.

The time and place of the composition of 1 John (as well as 2 John and 3 John) are approximately similar to those of John's gospel—around Ephesus in Asia Minor about the close of the first century. No doubt the destination of 1 John (as well as 2 John and 3 John) was one or more congregations in Asia Minor.

STUDY QUESTION 4

What type of false doctrine does 1 John refute? See 1 John 2:22; 4:2–3; 4:15; 5:5; 5:6. See also 1 John 1:8; 1:10. In what other writing does John refute this false doctrine?

The Occasion for 1 John

In brief, the situation is similar in part to what we saw in John's gospel—the church was confronted by a type of false teaching spread by certain Gnostics, who questioned the true humanity of Christ. 1 John points also to the result of the teaching of the Gnostics, who claim to have a superior knowledge of God. Since they believed that nothing the physical body does could tarnish the purity of the spirit, they felt free to live immoral lives.

These false teachers had arisen within the church and now were separated from the church (2:19; 4:4). But they were a threat to the church by trying to deceive Christians with their propaganda for their false doctrine (2:26; 3:7). They claimed to have the authority of the Holy Spirit (4:1) and no doubt used certain slogans to show a close relationship with God: "I know Him," "I abide in Him," "I am in the Light," "I love God" (2:4, 6, 9; 4:20).

Their denial of the humanity of Christ is evident in several statements of John: "Who is a liar but he who denies that Jesus is the Christ?" (2:22). "By this you know the Spirit of God: Every spirit that confesses that Jesus Christ has come in the flesh is of God, and every spirit that does not confess that Jesus Christ has come in the flesh is not of God" (4:2–3). "Whoever confesses that Jesus is the Son of God, God abides in him, and he in God" (4:15). "Who is he who overcomes the world, but he who believes that Jesus is the Son of God?" (5:5).

One verse deserves particular mention: "This is He who came by water and blood—Jesus Christ; not only by water, but by water and blood" (5:6). This passage is a direct refutation of the heresy of Cerinthus, who taught that a *human Jesus* was born and died on the cross, but a *heavenly Christ* descended on Him at His baptism and left Him before He died. John is emphasizing that Jesus Christ, God's Son, died on the cross when His blood was shed—that is, the same God-man died (blood) as the God-man who was baptized (water).

A related false teaching of the Gnostics was that their supposed superior knowledge allowed them to live immoral lives. They denied that any deeds of the physical body were really sinful, since they were "spiritual" believers. Again John is most clear in dealing with this false teaching. He states: "If we say that we have no sin, we deceive ourselves, and the truth is not in us. . . . If we say that we have not sinned, we make Him a liar, and His Word is not in us" (1:8, 10). In some respects the sinful lives of the Gnostics did not differ from the practices of unbelievers. So John can say: "They are of the world. Therefore they speak as of the world, and the world hears them" (4:5).

John meets the challenge of these false teachers in three ways: (1) He stresses the incarnation of Jesus Christ, who died in the flesh for the sins of human beings. (2) He shows that a Christian is a stranger in an alien world. (3) He emphasizes that the life of a Christian is centered in love—God's love for them and their love for each other.

Outline of 1 John

An expanded outline of 1 John should point out the themes of the document and also illustrate the spiral movement of the themes—a characteristic similar to what we have observed in the outline of John's gospel.

Test Yourselves

The Tests of the Christian Life Under Revelation
    I. Introduction: The revelation (1:1–4).
    II. The first standard: "God is light and in Him is no darkness at all" (1:5). Fellowship with God means "walking in the light" (1:5–2:28).
       A. The test of righteousness (1:8–2:6)
       B. The test of love (2:7–17)
       C. The test of true belief (2:18–28)

III. The second standard: "Now we are children of God" (3:2). Fellowship with God means being "children of God" (2:29–4:6).
   A. The test of righteousness (2:29–3:10)
   B. The test of love (3:11–24)
   C. The test of true belief (4:1–6)
IV. The third standard: "God is Love" (4:7–5:12). (Note how the three tests overlap as being inseparable.)
   A. The test of love (4:7–12, 16–21; 5:1–2)
   B. The test of true belief (4:13–15; 5:5–12)
   C. The test of righteousness (5:2–5)
V. Conclusion: The great certainties to which we hold (5:13–20).
   A. The certainty of eternal life (5:13)
   B. The certainty that our prayer is heard (5:14–17)
   C. The certainty that our life as God's children means separation from sin (5:18)
   D. The certainty that the Christian life means radical antagonism to the world, which is dominated by the Evil One (5:19)
   E. The certainty that in the Son of God we have the true revelation of the true God and eternal life (5:20)
VI. Closing admonition: "Keep yourselves from idols" (5:21).

STUDY QUESTION 5

Identify the addressee(s) of 2 John. What false teaching is refuted? Why does 2 John 10–11 warn against "hospitality"?

2 John

The language, literary style, and content of 2 John, together with the testimony of church tradition, lead to the conclusion that 2 John was written about the same time and by the same person as 1 John and the gospel. The false teaching against which John warns is the same as that in 1 John, as we see in the following statement: "Many deceivers have gone out into the world who do not confess Jesus Christ as coming in the flesh" (v. 7)—that is, the false teaching is Gnosticism.

In 2 John, however, the apostle is not addressing several churches but either a Christian lady or a congregation. As an aged apostle, perhaps the only apostle still alive, John refers to himself as "the elder" (v. 1). Since John does mention the name of an individual when he is writing to a person in 3 John (Gaius), many scholars believe that in 2 John the addressee, "the elect lady," is a church, that "her children" are the members of that church (v. 1), and the "children of your elect sister" (v. 13) are members of a sister church, probably John's own church. But we cannot be certain about the identification of the readers.

We see in 2 John the same emphasis as in 1 John on love (vv. 5, 6), the same stress on Jesus' incarnation (v. 7), the same term for the false teachers, "antichrist" (v. 7), and the same expression that no one can know the Father except through the incarnate Son (v. 9).

The unique characteristic of 2 John is the stern warning against furthering the activities of false teachers (vv. 10–11). Since missionaries were dependent on the hospitality of Christians, who would receive them as guests in their homes, hospitality to those teaching falsely would be equal to furthering false doctrine. This practice of hospitality is referred to also in 3 John.

Outline of 2 John

I. Greetings (vv. 1–3)
II. Walking in the truth (vv. 4–6)
III. Erroneous teachers (vv. 7–11)
    A. The spread of error should lead to self-examination (vv. 7–9).
    B. The false teachers should not be given hospitality (vv. 10–11).
IV. Conclusion: Plan to visit and greetings (vv. 12–13)

STUDY QUESTION 6

Why is Gaius commended in 3 John 2–8? Why is Diotrephes criticized in vv. 9–10? What part did Demetrius probably play (vv. 11–12)?

3 John

Again the apostle John refers to himself simply as "the elder" (v. 1). He is writing a letter to an individual named Gaius, which was a very common name in the Roman empire. In the New Testament we read of Gaius of Macedonia (Acts 19:29), Gaius of Corinth (1 Cor. 1:14; Rom. 16:23), and Gaius of Derbe (Acts 20:4).

John refers to this Gaius as "the beloved" in the salutation (v. 1) and several times in the body of the letter (vv. 2, 5, 11). He must have been a person of sterling Christian character, for he lived his life in active deeds of hospitality to messengers of the Gospel. Since he is not referred to as an official in the church, he probably was a lay member who assisted the missionary activities of the church.

The Occasion for 3 John

John apparently had received some report concerning the negative activity of a certain Diotrephes. When John had sent out missionaries to the surrounding area, Diotrephes refused to receive them and spoke out against the apostle himself. He no doubt was attempting to put himself in charge of that congregation. He even tried to put out of the church those members who were willing to receive the missionaries (vv. 9–10). Diotrephes engaged in this opposition in spite of a letter from John (v. 9—could this statement refer to 2 John?). In the face of such opposition Gaius befriended the missionaries, who on their return reported their experience to John. John now expresses to Gaius his appreciation for the warm reception of the missionaries and plans a personal visit to deal with the trouble (vv. 10, 14). Demetrius probably was the leader of the missionary party and the bearer of 3 John (v. 12).

Outline of 3 John

I. Greetings (v. 1)
II. Commendation of Gaius (vv. 2–8)
III. Criticism of Diotrephes (vv. 9–10)
IV. Commendation of Demetrius (vv. 11–12)
V. Conclusion: Plan to visit and greetings (vv. 13–14/15)

17. *Revelation: God's Grace in Symbolic Language*

Among the documents of the New Testament, Revelation is unique in that in it three types of literature come together. It has the form of a letter (1:4; 22:21), is a prophetic book, and uses "apocalyptic" features. "Apocalyptic" refers to the use of symbolism and imagery, similar to some parts of the Old Testament (Isaiah 24—27, Joel, Ezekiel, Daniel, Zechariah). Two extreme attitudes toward Revelation should be avoided: (1) that it cannot be understood and should be left alone, and (2) that it can be used to identify or predict events in secular history, such as those in the Middle East today.

STUDY QUESTION 1

What does Rev. 1:1–11 tell us about its author and addressees? What clues indicate that the same person wrote Revelation and the Fourth Gospel? See John 1:1, 14 and Rev. 19:13; see John 3:29 and Rev. 21:2, 9; 22:17; see John 19:34 and Rev. 1:7.

Author

The name of the writer is stated as John four times (1:1, 4, 9; 22:8). He is exiled on the island of Patmos (near Ephesus) because of his testimony concerning Jesus (1:9), and he records the vision he has been permitted to see (1:1) for the benefit of seven churches in Asia Minor (1:11).

The evidence of early church tradition strongly identifies the author as John the apostle, who wrote also the Fourth Gospel and the three epistles. Many scholars today question this identification on the basis of internal evidence. But internal evidence includes also numerous features that identify the author of Revelation as the same person who wrote the gospel and the three epistles.

Only in John's writings, for example, is Jesus called *Logos* or Word (John 1:1, 14; 1 John 1:1; Rev. 19:13). In Revelation Jesus is called Lamb 28 times; in the rest of the New Testament He is referred to as Lamb only in John's gospel (1:29, 36). Only in John's writings is Jesus depicted as the Bridegroom of the church (Rev. 21:2, 9; 22:17; John 3:29). Only John's gospel states that Jesus' side was pierced (John 19:34), a fact referred to in Rev. 1:7 with the identical verb—a different verb from that used in the Greek Old Testament (Septuagint) in Zech. 12:10.

It is true that the style and vocabulary of Revelation differ from John's gospel, but such variations should be expected in two distinctively different types of literature—a gospel account and a prophetic and apocalyptic document.

It is also true that John's gospel does not state his name as the writer, while Revelation does identify the author four times (1:1, 4, 9; 22:8). As we note this difference, we should recall a similar situation in the Old Testament. All the historical books of the Old Testament (except Nehemiah) are anonymous, while all the prophetic books give the names of the writers. John may be following the practice of Hebrew literature. In writing the history contained in the gospel he does not include his name, but as a prophet in Revelation he identifies himself as the author.

Addressees

The immediate addressees are seven churches in the Roman province of Asia (1:11): Ephesus, Smyrna, Pergamos, Thyatira, Sardis, Philadelphia, and Laodicea. The sequence in which these churches are listed may be the order in which the document is to be delivered. Of these seven churches only Ephesus is well known (Acts 19). Thyatira is the hometown of Lydia (Acts 16:14), and Laodicea is mentioned by Paul (Col. 4:15–16). The other names occur nowhere else in the New Testament.

STUDY QUESTION 2

The situation among the addressees.

A. *What situation is indicated in Rev. 2:6, 14–15?*

B. *What situation is indicated in Rev. 2:9; 3:9?*

C. *What situation is indicated in Rev. 1:4; 2:10, 13; 6:9–10; 16:6; 17:6; 18:24; 19:2; 20:4?*

D. *In which other New Testament books do we find similar situations?*

Occasion

According to Revelation there are three conflicts confronting these churches. They are being troubled by false teachers (2:6, 14–15). They are being harassed by Jews, referred to as the "synagogue of Satan" (2:9; 3:9). They are undergoing a persecution (1:9; 2:10), which has cost the lives of some Christians (2:13; 6:9–10) but has not yet reached its height (6:11). John is writing to strengthen the churches in their conflicts, internal and external, and to assure them of their hope in Christ for final victory over the powers of evil. We have noted similar conflicts in John's other writings—with Jews and false teaching (Gospel, 1 John, and 2 John) and with struggles for power (3 John). The unique conflict apparent in Revelation concerns persecution by the civil power of Rome.

STUDY QUESTION 3

What historical situation may be implied by the references to an image of a beast (or dragon) and its worship? See Rev. 13:4, 15–17; 14:9–11; 15:2; 16:2; 19:20; 20:4.

Domitian, the Roman emperor at that time (A.D. 81–96), insisted on the worship of himself as "Lord and God." His purpose no doubt was to unite the various religions in the Roman empire around a unifying theme, emperor worship. Some of the cities in the Roman province of Asia joined enthusiastically in the new cult. Pergamos, for example, had a temple called Augusteum, devoted to "the divine Augustus," where people worshiped the image of

Domitian. Refusal to worship the emperor's image was interpreted as disloyalty to Rome.

Christians, however, could not acknowledge Domitian as "Lord and God," for such honor and titles belong to Jesus alone (John 20:28). Persecution of Christians, therefore, broke out toward the end of Domitian's rule in the Roman province of Asia. John himself apparently was arrested and sent to exile on the island of Patmos (1:9). In Pergamos one Christian, Antipas by name, was put to death (2:13). In Smyrna (2:10) and in Philadelphia (3:10) the position of Christians became precarious. It appeared that believers in the province of Asia were in a life and death struggle against the power of Rome. Revelation contains repeated references to persecution (2:10, 13; 3:10; 6:9–10; 16:6; 17:6; 18:24; 19:2; 20:4). The conflict between Christianity and emperor worship is illustrated in the figure of a beast, his image, and the demand for worship (13:4, 15–17; 14:9–11; 15:2; 16:2; 19:20; 20:4).

STUDY QUESTION 4

The interpretation of Revelation.

A *Is Revelation to be taken as merely symbolic, or does it refer to events in the history of the church?*

B. *Are the visions beginning in chapter 4 to be taken as overlapping (in a spiral pattern) or as chronologically sequential?*

C. *Where else do we see a spiral pattern in the New Testament?*

Types of Interpretation

There have been four basic approaches to the interpretation of Revelation. We shall describe each briefly:

1. *Preterist View:* The word "preterist" comes from a Latin term that means "past." This interpretation limits Revelation to events in the first century A.D. It assumes that all the visions are based on historical events that had already occurred. These past events are described in the form of predictions.

2. *Futurist View:* This approach assumes that all the visions beginning in chapter 4 describe events that are to happen imme-

diately before the second coming of Christ and those connected with a "millennial kingdom" of a thousand years. Such a view sees a period of "rapture" and a "great tribulation" of seven years.

3. *Idealist View:* This interpretation assumes that there is no connection between the visions and historical facts. It sees in Revelation only general principles, portraying the struggle between the church and the world and assuring the triumph of God's kingdom in the end.

4. *Historicist View:* This approach assumes that Revelation presents a continuous forecast of the history of the church from apostolic days to Jesus' second coming. It assumes that each successive vision describes a sequence of events that follow one after the other chronologically.

There is some truth in each of these interpretations, but each one by itself is one-sided and misleading. It is true, according to the preterist view, that the background of Revelation is rooted in the contemporary events of the day. The seven letters in chapters 2 and 3 do refer to the situations in those churches at the time of writing. It is also true, according to the futurist view, that Revelation includes events immediately preceding Jesus' second coming (but the visions are not limited to that time in history). It is true, according to the idealist view, that Revelation teaches general principles (but it also has a more direct relevance to the history of the church). It is true, according to the historicist view, that Revelation describes the general course of church history (but it is not meant to be a blueprint of past and future events).

It is important to note that each vision (after chapter 3) describes the entire period from the apostolic age to the second coming of Christ. Instead of being chronologically sequential, the visions are parallel presentations of the same basic truths. Each vision accents a new aspect of the same theme. The visions, then, have a cumulative effect and are similar to the spiral pattern that we saw in John's gospel (prolog and body of the gospel) and in 1 John (outline).

Perhaps a good approach to our study of Revelation is to give a summarizing outline.

STUDY QUESTION 5

Students of Scripture usually outline Revelation on the basis of the seven visions.

A. **Identify the seven visions in Rev. 2:1–3:22; 4:1–8:1; 8:2–11:19; 12:1–15:4; 15:5–16:21; 17:1–20:15; 21:1–22:5.**

B. **What other New Testament writing emphasizes the number seven?**

Outline

Introduction (1:1–20). The first chapter presents the name of the author, the addressees (seven churches), and a vision of Jesus Christ. The living Christ is described in all His power and glory as the Master of life and death and human destiny.

First Vision: Seven Letters (2:1–3:22). Although the letters are to particular congregations, the message is meant for the entire church. There are dangers from within as well as from without. The purpose of these letters is encouragement in loyalty to Jesus Christ in the face of internal and external trials. Christians who were suffering persecution are given hope of the glory that they would finally attain; the persecutors also would receive their appropriate reward.

Second Vision: Seven Seals (4:1–8:1). The scene now changes from earth to heaven. God is sitting on His throne. His splendor is compared to precious stones, a brilliant rainbow, and spectacular sights. Thus the picture of the struggling congregations fades before the sublime vision of God's throne. Four living creatures surround that throne; they represent God's power (lion), strength (ox), wisdom (man), and mobility (flying eagle). These four living creatures and 24 elders (representing His faithful people) join in giving God glory, honor, and thanks.

God holds in His right hand a scroll with seven seals (5:1), containing the world's destiny between Jesus' ascension and His second coming. There will be war, civil strife, famine, pestilence, and disease; there also will be slain martyrs. But regardless of the disasters, God is in control. His love and care for His people never fail. Certain cataclysmic events signify God's day of judgment, when the present physical world will come to an end and the wicked will be judged (6:12–17). But the forces of destruction will be restrained for God to place His mark of ownership on those who belong to Him. Their number, 144,000 (12 x 12 x 1000), is symbolic of a great multitude (7:1–8:1).

Third Vision: Seven Trumpets (8:2–11:19). The seven trumpets follow the same pattern as the seven seals. The trumpets indicate God's judgments, which now are more intense but do not bring total destruction. The first four calamities affect the world of nature—earth, sea, water, and the heavens (8:2–13).

The fifth and the sixth calamities affect mankind. God unleashes huge locusts, which are confined to a time limit and have no power to touch God's people. He then unleashes a large cavalry, which has power to kill—but within limits. In spite of these warnings, people refuse to amend their lives—a picture characteristic of the world (9:1–21).

Between the sixth and the seventh trumpets is inserted an interlude, as there is between the sixth and the seventh seals. This interlude of two visions (10:1–11; 11:1–13) describes the preservation of God's people from the forces of evil. Then the seventh trumpet announces that "the kingdoms of this world have become the kingdoms of our Lord and of His Christ, and He shall reign forever and ever!" (11:14–18).

Fourth Vision: Woman and Dragon (12:1–15:4). These chapters contain encouragement for a persecuted church. The woman is God's chosen people and bearer of the promised Messiah (12:5) and of the church (12:17). The dragon is Satan, who desires the destruction of God's people. The main message is that Satan, although strong and powerful, has been overcome by Christ and is destined to destruction. The church will triumph and is under the protection of God (12:1–17).

Two beasts, representing the Roman empire and emperor worship, are hostile to God's people and act as Satan's agents (13:1–18). But victory belongs to God's people, who follow the Lamb (14:1) and have been redeemed (14:4). God will judge the world, and His people will sing the song of the Lamb (14:6–15:4).

Fifth Vision: Seven Bowls (15:5–16:21). The seven bowls of wrath contain seven plagues, recalling the plagues that befell Egypt at the time of the Exodus. These disasters are warnings of what will befall those who oppose God.

Sixth Vision: God's Final Triumph (17:1–20:15). This section depicts God's ultimate victory over evil, which is symbolized by a harlot (17:1), also called Babylon (17:5). Babylon, a center of opposition to God's people in the Old Testament, has its counterpart in Rome, a city built on seven hills (17:9). In Rome Christians were thrown to lions and burnt alive under Nero and now are commanded to engage in emperor worship under Domitian. The king (beast) who was and is not and will be the eighth (17:11) could refer to the legend of the return of Nero, which developed during the reign of Domitian. The forces of evil will make war on the Lamb, but the Lamb will conquer (17:14).

Babylon's doom is so certain that it is said to have occurred already: "Babylon the great is fallen" (18:2). God's people need full assurance concerning the doom of Babylon, so its destruction is described at great length. First it is announced by two angels (18:1–8). Then there is lamentation over its fall by kings, merchants, and sailors (18:9–20). There follows a symbolic act by an angel—the throwing of a stone into the sea (18:21–24)—symbolizing the fall of Babylon. In heaven there is rejoicing over the doom of Babylon (19:1–10), which includes a wedding feast of Christ and His bride, the church (19:6–10). Christ is now victorious over the two beasts, henchmen of Satan (19:11–21).

Finally, Satan himself is overcome, released for a time, and bound again forever and ever (20:1–10). There follows the final and universal judgment (20:11–15). This chapter, with references to a thousand years, is frequently misinterpreted as if there will be a "millennium" (an earthly rule of a thousand years) before Christ's second coming. What it describes is the overthrow of Satan in two stages. The first stage, the binding of Satan for a thousand years, occurred at the time of the Messiah. The thousand-year period symbolizes the reign of Christ from His ascension to His second coming. This reign is not apparent to the world, which refuses to recognize Christ as Lord of the universe, so it may be called a "hidden reign." At Jesus' second coming, His reign and eternal power will be evident to all. Then will occur the general resurrection, when all people will be judged before God. (Apparently Satan will be allowed to make a final assault on God's people before he is bound forever.)

Seventh Vision: God's New World (21:1–22:5). After the destruction of all evil, including death, there will arise a new world— a new heaven, a new earth, and a new Jerusalem. Nothing will spoil the new world—no sorrow, no pain, no sin. But the positive side is even more important—eternal and perfect relationship with God, who is always there and brings peace, freedom, and security. The description in earthly terms symbolizes incredible magnificence. There will be no need for a temple, for God Himself will live among His people.

Conclusion (22:6–21). John affirms that what he has written is true, as witnessed by the angel (22:6–11) and by Jesus (22:12–17); he also warns against tampering with these words (22:18–19).

STUDY QUESTION 6

What lessons do we learn from Revelation?

Lessons from Revelation

The last book of the New Testament teaches lessons similar to those in the rest of Scripture. God is in control of world history and of the fortunes of His people. He keeps a watchful eye on them when they are persecuted. Satan and the forces of evil, although troubling God's people in this world, have been conquered and will be bound permanently at the second coming of Christ. At that time the final victory of Christ, hidden for the time being, will become evident to all, when He ushers in a new world for His people from all nations to endure into eternity.

Epilog

We trust that this volume not only has increased *pleasure* and *information* in reading the New Testament, but above all has begun a training in a method of studying Scripture that we have called *reading for understanding.*

These chapters have provided merely a beginning in the reading of the New Testament for understanding. A continuation of this method should result in discovering many more clues in the documents that will enhance the understanding of God's message to Christians.

While the study, and even memorization, of Bible passages out of context, as in a catechism, is important, a grasp of the whole picture of God's message in its entire context (including the Old Testament) gives added meaning, understanding, comfort, and hope—especially in our current age of moral permissiveness and theological confusion.

If these pages have opened eyes to the endless possibilities of understanding more about God's grace and His will for His followers, we give all praise to God the Father for our election from eternity, to God the Son for His sacrificial life, death, resurrection, and ascension in our behalf, and to God the Holy Spirit for working faith in our hearts, thus leading and strengthening us in the eternal truths of the Gospel—that we may anticipate with confident assurance our glorious reunion with the Lamb in all eternity.

Soli Deo Gloria